Vegetarian Chin

素食清歡

Vegetarian Chinese Soul Food

Deliciously Doable Ways to Cook Greens, Tofu, and Other Plant-Based Ingredients

HSIAO-CHING CHOU

Author of *Chinese Soul Food*

Photography by Clare Barboza

SASQUATCH BOOKS
SEATTLE

For "The Cousins": Meilee, Shen, Jackson,
Lucie, Sadie, Duncan, and Fletcher.
Eat your vegetables, kids!

Introduction 11

Key Ingredients, Techniques, and Equipment 15

Dumplings 64

Dim Sum and Small Bites 80

Soups and Braises 106

Stir-Fries 128

Steamed Dishes 156

Rice and Noodles 176

Tofu 196

Eggs 224

Salads and Pickles 240

Acknowledgments 259

Index 263

Recipe List

64 **DUMPLINGS**

72 Classic Dumpling Dough

74 Gluten-Free Dumpling Dough

76 Tofu and Spinach Filling

77 Plant-Based "Beef" with Asparagus Filling

78 Dumpling Dipping Sauce

80 **DIM SUM AND SMALL BITES**

85 Crystal Dumplings with Squash and Peas

89 Flaky Ribbon Pancakes

92 Spring Rolls

95 Soup Dumplings

99 Sticky Rice in Lotus Leaf

103 Steamed Vegetable Baozi

105 Red Bean Soup

106 **SOUPS AND BRAISES**

109 Vegetable Broth

110 Ginger-Red Date Broth

111 Braised Chinese Cabbage and Fried Shallots

113 Mian Pian Soup

114 Hot-and-Sour Soup with Dried Lily Flowers

115 Braised Daikon

116 Chinese Purple Seaweed and Tofu Soup

118 Rice Cake Soup with Vegetables

119 Vegetarian Wonton Soup

123 Sweet Corn Soup

124 Taiwanese Cabbage and Tomato Soup with Bean Thread Noodles

127 Braised Bamboo Shoots and Shiitake Mushrooms

128 **STIR-FRIES**

131 Garlic Yam Leaf

132 Yu Choy with Fried Shallots

135 Crisp Vegetables with Lily Flowers

137 Ginger-Scallion Pea Shoots

138 "BLT" - Beech Mushrooms, Lettuce, and Tomato

141 Wok-Seared Edamame and Corn

142 Taiwanese Cabbage with Garlic and Chili

144 Dry-Fried Brussels Sprouts

147 Chinese Mustard Greens with Shishito Peppers

148 Gai Lan with Oyster Mushrooms

150 Hot-and-Sour Celery, Carrots, and Bean Sprouts

151 Cauliflower Rice with Eggplant and Gai Lan

152 Shen's Wok-Seared Broccoli with Jalapeños

154 Lucky 8 Stir-Fry

156 **STEAMED DISHES**

159 Savory Mushrooms with Rice Powder

160 Simply Steamed Baby Bok Choy

163 Asparagus with Shiitake and Oyster Mushrooms

164 Gai Lan with Sesame Sauce

165 Cucumber and Wood Ear Mushrooms

166 Cauliflower with Edamame, Fried Onions, and Garlic

169 Winter Melon with Smoked Salt

170 Eggplant with Black Bean Garlic Sauce

173 Chinese Cabbage Heart with Goji Berries

174 Sweet Potatoes with Chili-Shallot Jam

176 **RICE AND NOODLES**

179 Steamed Rice

180 Fried Brown Rice with Oyster Mushrooms and Greens

183 Mung Bean Congee

184 Rice Cake with Mixed Vegetables

187 Rice Vermicelli with Vegetables

188 Simple Stir-Fried Noodles

191 Vegetable Noodle Soup

192 Da Lu Noodles

193 Simple Vegetable Fried Rice

194 Hong Kong–Style Crispy Noodles

196 **TOFU**

199 Kung Pao Tofu Puffs

203 Spiced Tofu with Leeks and Cabbage

204 Carrots and Celery with Spiced Tofu

206 Meatless Ma Po Tofu

209 Tofu Rolls

211 Braised Tofu and Vegetables

212 Tofu, Peas, and Carrots

213 Tofu Ribbon Slaw

214 Seared Tofu with Baby Bok Choy

217 Sichuan Pepper Salt Fried Tofu

218 Savory Soy Milk with Youtiao and Shao Bing

224 **EGGS**

227 Egg Bing with Onions and Bean Sprouts

228 Dad's Steamed Eggs with Tomatoes

231 Scrambled Eggs with Chinese Mustard Greens

232 Zucchini Egg Crepe

235 Wok-Fried Egg in Onion Oil

236 Home-Style Egg Foo Yung with Curry Gravy

238 Stir-Fried Eggs with Bean Thread Noodles and Wood Ear

239 Mu Shu Vegetables

240 **SALADS AND PICKLES**

243 Chili Radish in Soy Sauce

244 Pickled Cucumber in Soy Sauce

245 Fermented Mustard Greens with Garlic

246 Fermented Chinese Cabbage and Goji Berries

247 Sweet-and-Sour Cucumber and Carrots

248 Cloud Ear Mushrooms with Pickled Chilis

251 Chopped Taiwanese Cabbage with Peanuts and Chili Oil

252 Chinese Cabbage Slaw

253 Celery and Carrot Slaw

254 Seaweed Salad

257 Ma La Succotash

Introduction

Vegetables are essential in Chinese cooking. Whether a mound of stir-fried greens, a burbling clay pot of tofu and cabbage, or a side of spicy pickles, vegetable dishes are put together with as much thought as any meat or seafood dish. Balance of seasonality, flavors, textures, and sometimes curative properties guides the preparation. Even those who eat meat are biased toward having an abundance of vegetables. Many dishes include meat only as an accompaniment.

Being vegetarian in the Chinese culture is not perceived as a character flaw. Not only is vegetarianism accepted, but the industry for producing plant-based products and meat substitutes has a long history. That is due in large part to Chinese Buddhist monks and nuns who adhere to a vegan diet that also excludes pungent ingredients, such as alcohol, garlic, onions, leeks, and chives. Not all followers of Buddhism subscribe to a vegetarian diet, however. But temple vegetarian cuisine is well known and even revered. Culturally, meat has always been considered a luxury because it's expensive. During Lunar New Year, serving a broad selection of meats and seafood represents wealth, abundance, and good fortune. Historically, the advent of meat and seafood substitutes made from plant-based ingredients has meant that those who couldn't afford meat or those who have chosen to be vegetarian for health or religious reasons could also share in the symbolism, especially when it comes to "lucky foods" served during the Lunar New Year reunion feast. Using bean curd and wheat gluten to create meat substitutes goes back to imperial China and has been around for over a thousand years.

A NOTE ON PORTION SIZE

There are so many factors that affect whether a portion size is right for any one person. A pint of ice cream, in my opinion, does not have four servings! When it comes to the portion sizes for the recipes in this book, they're based on the assumption that you'll be serving several dishes family-style. Some dishes, such as noodles and fried rice, are bulkier. Others, such as stir-fried pea shoots, start as a messy mound of greens and then cook down to a fraction of itself. Usually, if you have a group of four people, I suggest making three or four dishes and a soup. The flip side is that if you are cooking for one or two, many of these dishes are easy to scale down.

I have noticed recently at the Chinese market where I shop here in the Seattle area that there are more products marketed toward vegetarians. For example, the same hoisin sauce that I've always used now has a bottle label listing it as vegetarian. It's the same naturally vegetarian sauce, just a different label. My mother and I scrutinized the label and finally surmised that the "vegetarian" designation potentially has to do with the fact that "hoisin" is *hai xian* in Mandarin, which means "seafood," and adding the word "vegetarian" was a clear message that the *hai xian* sauce does not contain seafood. Likewise, a bottle of Chinese black vinegar had a sitting Buddha figure on its label that also proclaimed that the vinegar is vegetarian. Again, we suspect it's a direct way to signal to vegetarians, especially Buddhist vegetarians, that this vinegar is not flavored with any forbidden pungent ingredients.

For me, a meal is never complete without at least one vegetable dish. My produce drawers are always stocked with Chinese cabbage, baby bok choy, *gai lan* (Chinese broccoli), Chinese mustard greens, yu choy, and a revolving cast of other familiar vegetables—carrots, celery, kale, lettuce, cucumber, broccoli, cauliflower, potatoes, and such—that cater to our cravings. At a moment's notice—or in the time it takes to make a pot of rice—I can have a sumptuous meal on the table with platters of greens, eggplant, mushrooms, and tofu. Delicate, hearty, savory, pungent, and crunchy all coexist in their individuality and intersections.

The diversity of vegetables and plant foods is dizzying. On occasion, I teach an Asian greens cooking class, where I display a dozen kinds of uncooked leafy greens paired with their respective stir-fried versions. Students then sample each vegetable, and the deliciousness is always a revelation. I will never not delight in the looks on people's faces when they taste discovery.

In the Chinese language, the word for "vegetables" is *cai* (also spelled *tsai, choy,* or *choi*). It's a broad term that covers a world of greens as a category, as well as the specific members of this succulent family: bok choy, yu choy, *gai choy, qincai, ong choy,* and so on. *Cai* is also a general term for "dish"—as in "What dishes should we eat today?" or "What dishes should I cook today?"

I love the preciseness and expansiveness of the term *cai*: It means one thing and everything, so context is important for determining whether you're referring to a specific vegetable or a meal. If you're not used to such conciseness in language, it may cause confusion. To me, there's freedom in this ability to shapeshift, which we certainly can extend to the versatility of the Chinese *way* with all forms of vegetables and plant foods.

When I talk about a *way* with vegetables, my intention is to convey an approach rather than rigid rules and recipes. The alchemy of a searing wok, a splash of oil, a

A NOTE ON DESSERTS AND WINE

The Chinese tend to serve fruit at the end of a meal. Desserts or sweets are usually reserved for snacks or afternoon treats. If I serve desserts at a meal, it's likely a cake or pie from one of my favorite dessert cookbooks or store-bought ice cream. Don't get me wrong, I love desserts and love to bake. But Chinese desserts are often acquired tastes for my Western friends and family. Sweetened Red Bean Soup (page 105) is a dessert that my mother and I would enjoy, but it wouldn't satisfy what my kids and husband would consider a post-dinner treat.

Trying to pair wines with the myriad hot-sour-salty-sweet-umami flavors that a Chinese meal balances among a number of dishes is an exercise in futility. What goes with one dish will most certainly fall flat for another. This is why people find it's easier to drink beer with Chinese food. Sweet dessert wines fare better than dry wines, but wine aficionados frown on the idea of having sweet wine for an entire meal.

Fellow author Fuchsia Dunlop, who has written several books on Sichuan and other regional Chinese cuisines, published an article where she suggested that wines be treated like any other dish in the complement of dishes within a meal. The idea is that you might take a bite of spicy, garlicky eggplant, followed by a sip of a light broth and then a sip of wine, without worrying whether the wine goes specifically with the eggplant. This resonates. Appreciate the wine for its own flavor profile as you would any other dish on the table. Grape-wine culture is relatively new to the Chinese, so it has taken an outsider who has developed an insider's view to bridge the perspectives. Dunlop also has said that there's a burgeoning trend of pairing whiskey with Chinese food. I wouldn't be surprised if that triggers a spate of dinner events at a hotspot near you.

mess of fresh greens, and a dash of soy sauce delivers a quintessential flavor that roots your palate in this approach. From that point of reference, a kaleidoscope of dazzling combinations can emerge at the twist of inspiration. A recipe with specific amounts isn't as important as understanding the nature of vegetables and the support characters that make them sing.

As I've become more attuned to the wisdom that comes from lived experiences, I have realized that my taste preferences have shed thrill-seeking for more focused flavors. I do enjoy adding a dollop of fire from my menagerie of chili sauces to many dishes, but I also understand the value of restraint. I will always encourage you to experiment with building complexity in your cooking, and I will also always remind you to appreciate the elemental. Subtle flavors in food are not boring.

The way to cook vegetables, for me, is about exploring flavors without heroics at the stove. I remain firm in my belief that everyday cooking should be accessible and forgiving. As with this book's predecessor, my goal is to ground you in everyday Chinese home cooking, with hopes you will consider developing your own Chinese kitchen.

HOW TO USE THIS BOOK

This is a book about cooking with assorted Asian vegetables and plant-based ingredients. You may or may not be familiar with these ingredients. If you are, you likely have your own preferred ways to work with them. If you aren't, welcome to my kitchen! There are a few ways to use this book. In some respects, it's the continuation of my first book, *Chinese Soul Food*. My one wish (regret is too strong a word) is that I had included more vegetable dishes. If you have the first book, consider this the companion. You can cook across them both for any given meal. That said, *Vegetarian Chinese Soul Food* stands on its own—though it doesn't have as much of my personal narrative woven into its pages.

You will be able to make complete meals that are vegetarian or naturally vegan. Other than the recipes in the egg chapter, there are several other recipes that contain eggs as a secondary ingredient. You can omit the egg if you wish. I have not tested the recipes in the egg chapter with vegan eggs, so I can't speak to the quality of substitutions. I'm not a vegetarian and I'm not an expert in Buddhist vegetarian cuisine. I cook a lot of vegetables because they are an essential part of a meal that's balanced in flavors, textures, and nutrition.

Finally, you can also use this collection of recipes as a resource for vegetable sides. You'll find that many of the dishes—the Dry-Fried Brussels Sprouts (page 144) or Shen's Wok-Seared Broccoli with Jalapeños (page 152), for example—could easily pair with a weekend roast or a holiday meal.

Key Ingredients, Equipment, and Techniques

A cookbook of any kind is a wonderland of flavor adventures. Familiar ingredients become new in unexpected combinations or step out from the shadows into featured roles. I have tried to create a balance of recipes that use readily available ingredients with a few that invite you to try ingredients and perhaps equipment that will require a trip to an Asian market.

The items listed under Core Pantry Ingredients are all used in the recipes in this book. It is far from a comprehensive collection of potential ingredients you could use to make this food, however. I encourage you to experiment. Chinese cabbage and savoy cabbage, for example, aren't interchangeable per se, but flavors that work with Chinese cabbage would certainly work with savoy.

By the way, not all Asian markets are the same. You are more likely to find a wider selection of Chinese produce, pantry items, and soy sauces (see An Ode to Soy Sauce, page 43) in a Chinese market, such as 99 Ranch Market, versus a Japanese market, such as Uwajimaya in the Pacific Northwest, or the national Korean chain Hmart. These are also not to be confused with Vietnamese, Filipino, or any number of culture-specific markets. You will likely find the most crossover in the produce and protein sections. But when it comes to pantry items, such as sauces, grains, and dried goods, the stores will lean more toward their respective cultural origins. Larger chain markets have better capacity to offer a broader spectrum of ingredients, but it's not guaranteed that you'll be able to find specific Chinese items in, say, a Filipino market.

Core Pantry Ingredients

If you stock these ingredients in your pantry, you can make many dishes in this book. I benefit from ample storage, so I can keep the cabinets stocked with a generous assortment of shelf-stable ingredients. If you have tighter quarters, start with the curated list of ingredients (marked with an asterisk) and try recipes that incorporate them. To the best of my abilities, I have included ingredients that are used in multiple recipes so that you aren't stuck with an ingredient that's used just once. There are a couple of one-off items, but most are used in more than one recipe.

BEAN SAUCE AND SWEET BEAN SAUCE: Bean sauce (also called bean paste) is made from fermented yellow soybeans and is used a variety of dishes. It's also an ingredient in hoisin sauce and the so-called duck sauce. Sweet bean sauce or paste (also called sweet flour sauce) is made from flour, sugar, salt, and fermented yellow soybeans left over from making soy sauce. It's used to flavor and thicken various sauces for noodles or stir-fries. Black bean sauce and black bean garlic sauce are made from black soybeans. The garlic-flavored version can be quite pungent, but a spoonful can completely transform a dish.

*BEAN THREAD: Also called cellophane, glass, vermicelli, or saifun noodles, bean thread is made out of mung bean starch and potato starch. Look for the term "bean thread" on the package because, if you're not familiar, it's easy to confuse it with rice vermicelli or rice stick. Soak the bundle of noodles in warm tap water for five to ten minutes to become pliable. In Asian markets, it's common to see bean thread in packs of eight bundles that are wrapped in a pink net bag. They store indefinitely in the cabinet.

*CHILI BEAN SAUCE OR PASTE: This is made from fermented chilies and fava beans or soybeans, depending on where it's produced. The spice level can vary dramatically depending on the type of chilies used. A good, mass-market brand is Lee Kum Kee, which has a range of chili bean sauces including some with chili oil.

CHILI OIL: Bottled chili oils can easily go rancid. It's not hard to make your own. Chili oil usually is made by heating a neutral-flavored oil and adding it to ground red chili peppers or crushed red pepper. Sometimes, other spices, such as Sichuan peppercorns, may be included. (See recipe, page 207.)

CHINESE PURPLE SEAWEED

DRIED KELP

DRIED KELP SQUARES

SLICED SEAWEED

*CHILI SAUCE OR PASTE: There are many brands of chili sauce that have varying degrees of spiciness, so you may have to try different ones to find the one that hits the right level of spice for you. Some chili sauces also contain garlic, fermented black beans, or sugar.

DRIED CHINESE RED DATES OR JUJUBES: The fruit of a shrub, dried dates are used in health tonics and are believed to help balance your body's *qi*. The dates can be used in condiments, savory foods, sweets, liquor, or eaten as a snack. When buying, look for plump dates that aren't too shriveled. You can get small to large dates. Do choose the dates that are packed in vacuum-packed bags, which tend to look livelier. The flesh is sweet and there's a seed inside. I add them to my vegetable broth to help balance the flavor. I also will add a couple of dates to a mug of hot water with a few goji berries as a warming beverage.

*DRIED KELP: Kelp is used in soups, salads, and stir-fries. You can buy them as large sheets, thin strips, or bite-size squares. Having precut pieces makes it easier to drop them directly into soups. Buying kelp can be confusing because there are so many types, and the labels on the packages aren't always easily understood. I try to get smaller packages with pieces that are manageable to use. That at least helps to narrow down the options. **Prep:** If you have kelp sheets, soak in warm tap water for about thirty minutes, or until softened enough to cut to desired size or shape. You will have to rinse the slime off the surface and blanch the seaweed for one to two minutes before using for a cold salad.

DRIED LILY FLOWERS: Dried lily flowers are also called tiger lily buds or golden needles. They're often used in Buddhist vegetarian cooking and also for medicinal purposes to

WHERE TO SHOP

Asian markets abound. Depending on where you live, you may have more (or fewer) options than most. In major urban areas, there usually are dedicated Chinese markets and that will be your best bet for specialty ingredients. A national chain is 99 Ranch Market (99Ranch.com). For woks and assorted kitchenware, including Chinese glass or ceramic pickling jars, visit WokShop .com or drop by the legendary shop the next time you visit San Francisco. For specialty Sichuan spices and condiments, visit TheMalaMarket.com. This is where you can get premium Sichuan peppercorns. As always, you can find many tools at sites such as Amazon.com.

treat nerves or coughs. The flower should be soaked for about thirty minutes and the hard tip needs to be trimmed before using.

*DRIED SHIITAKE MUSHROOM: Dried shiitake come in different varieties and sizes from mini to large. The more prized types are small, thick, and have a crackle-like pattern on the cap. They're called *hua gu*, which translates to "flower mushroom," and can be expensive. The other, more utilitarian type of shiitake is called *xiang gu*, or "fragrant mushroom." The caps are thinner, darker, and smoother. I prefer the fragrant shiitake for the flavor they add to soups and stir-fries. For the purposes of the recipes in this book, a medium shiitake mushroom is one that has a cap measuring roughly 1½ to 2 inches in diameter. If you get bigger or smaller mushrooms, then adjust the amount accordingly. **Prep:** Soak in warm water for at least 2 hours or until rehydrated.

*DRIED WOOD EAR AND CLOUD EAR FUNGUS: This crunchy, mildly flavored fungus is used for texture in any number of dishes and for its purported health benefits. Much of the wood ear that's available is cultivated. It is possible to purchase wild ones, but it's hard to tell based on packaging unless you can read the Chinese characters on the label. There are many varieties and sizes of wood ear, which can make it confusing to buy—and to measure for a recipe. The larger ones, when rehydrated, must be cut. Smaller ones can be used whole. The cloud ear fungus is a type of wood ear, but it's typically grown at higher altitudes and are from the Yunnan region. The *yun* in Yunnan means "cloud." So *yun er* (雲耳) is cloud ear, and *mu er* (木耳) is wood ear. **Prep:** Soak in warm water for twenty to thirty minutes, or until reconstituted. If whole, trim the stem end (the white, stump-like knob) and cut into desired size. Precut strips can be used right away.

FERMENTED TOFU: Fermented tofu is pungent and has a funky flavor akin to stinky cheese. It's often served as a condiment for congee, but it's a great addition in marinades, where its pungency enhances the overall flavor but also is tamed by other ingredients. Look for jars of fermented tofu in the refrigerated section in Asian markets. If it's the spicy version, the tofu will be submerged in flaming-red chili oil.

FRIED SHALLOTS: Fried shallots add another flavor dimension and crunchy texture to savory recipes. They're widely available in large packs or plastic jars at Asian markets, though it's hard to be sure the contents are fresh. If the shallots seem a little old, you can refresh them by toasting them in a small skillet over low heat for about 2 minutes.

SIZE ROULETTE

Baby bok choy isn't always so baby. Wood ear and cloud ear mushrooms can be nickel-size or the size of your hand. Shiitake mushrooms have a similar range. It's hard to describe such variability within the ingredient list of a recipe without bogging down the reader's ability to scan the list. So you end up with something like "6 medium shiitake mushrooms" without much reference for what constitutes a medium shiitake mushroom. Having a visual sense of the range of sizes will help you assess the relative dimensions of the ingredients you're buying. The least vague way to quantify such ingredients is by weight. Half a cup of small wood ear mushrooms is easy enough to measure, but what's the equivalent in large wood ears, which don't fit into a measuring cup the same way? However, half an ounce of wood ear is half an ounce. Bottom line: Use this image as a reference and get a digital scale.

DRIED THIN
NOODLES

DRIED MEDIUM
NOODLES

DRIED SLICED NOODLES

BEAN THREAD

RICE VERMICELLI

I have had good luck with the Hsin Tung Yang brand. If you have time, you can make your own. (See recipe, page 132.)

HOISIN SAUCE: Made from yellow beans, sugar, vinegar, salt, and many other seasonings according to the manufacturer's recipe, hoisin sauce is often used as a condiment or mixed with other sauces to flavor stir-fries. Most people are familiar with hoisin because it's a constant companion at pho restaurants. It has crossed over to the mainstream and sometimes makes appearances in non-Asian recipes too. I use hoisin sparingly because it can add too much sweetness to a dish.

LOTUS LEAF (DRIED): These massive leaves are used to make the dim sum favorite sticky rice in lotus leaf. The dried leaves look like giant earthy-green fans. A pack will provide more leaves than you likely will be able to use in a year or two—unless you make this dish for a big party. When buying, look for leaves that still have some vibrancy. Because of the way the leaves are folded, you will see the underside, which is a light-khaki color. But you will be able to see some of the earthy-green color of the top side of the leaves peek out. If the leaves are past their prime, they will look dull and brittle and possibly have lots of cracks or holes. **Prep:** Soak the leaves in water until they become pliable, about one hour.

*NOODLES (WHEAT): The number of styles of dried and fresh wheat noodles can be dizzying, and I highly recommend visiting a Chinese market to explore the options. If you buy only the "Chinese noodles" that are sold in regular supermarkets, you will miss out on the diversity of fresh and dried noodles that are available. In general, I keep a family-size box of thin or medium dried noodles in the cabinet. Then, as inspiration strikes, I might try a new-to-me brand or type of dried or fresh noodles. For example, the hand-cut-style dried noodles are wide, thin noodles that have wavy edges. These provide a different kind of texture and mouthfeel, which is an aspect that a Chinese cook considers in addition to the taste of the sauce or soup. This is separate from the rice noodles that I also stock in my pantry. **Prep:** Cook according to package directions.

PICKLED CHINESE MUSTARD GREENS: Often used as a condiment for noodles or different types of steamed buns, pickled Chinese mustard greens can be added to soups and stir-fries. The pickled greens come in a plastic, shelf-stable pouch and usually can be found in the dry goods or refrigerated section at an Asian market. Rinse the greens before using. You also can ferment your own. (See recipe, page 245.)

RED CHILI PEPPERS (DRIED): There are many types of dried red chili peppers. Asian markets sell generic ones and the packaging may not reveal the specific variety of pepper. You can use Mexican chile de arbol or similar, if you'd like.

RED CHILI POWDER: Chinese- or Korean-style chili powder (used in kimchi making) is what you use to make chili oil. The powder typically comes in one-pound packs or larger. Unlike the finely ground chili powder you might use for making a barbecue rub or a bowl of bean chili, the Asian chili powders are much coarser. Stored in an airtight container, it should last at least six months. To make chili oil, see recipe on page 207. Over time, the oil will intensify. Keep the oil in an airtight container and store in the pantry.

*RICE: Rice is very personal. Whether the rice is short-, medium-, or long-grain, or white or brown, the choice depends on what flavor and texture appeal to you, as well as the cost. A good "all-purpose" rice is jasmine, which I happened to grow up eating. In Asian markets, the jasmine rice is most likely from Thailand. It's fragrant and delicious. I personally enjoy the glutinous quality of medium-grain Japanese rices. What has influenced that preference is the fact that a major Asian market in Seattle, where I live, is Japan-centric. Choose the rice that suits you. Recipe note: For the Sticky Rice in Lotus Leaf (page 99), you will need to buy sweet rice, which will be clear on the label. If it's a Thai brand, it will be labeled "Thai sticky rice." **Prep:** Cook according to chosen method and type of rice.

RICE NOODLES (DRIED): Also called rice stick or rice vermicelli, these noodles resemble angel hair pasta in fineness. Stir-frying is the most common method of usage, though it's delicious in soups too. **Prep:** Soak in warm tap water until pliable.

RICE WINE: Rice wine is a common ingredient in Chinese cooking. There are two main types that are used in cooking. Michiu (*mi* = rice and *chiu* = alcohol) is clear. Shaoxing wine is amber-colored and comes specifically from the Shaoxing region in China. It's not imperative to have this wine for cooking the recipes in this book. If you need just a splash, you can also use whatever dry, white wine you have on hand.

*SESAME OIL: Sesame oil is intended as a finishing touch in a cooked dish or mixed into a filling, marinade, or sauce. It's not meant to be used as a cooking oil. (I have seen some recipes call for using sesame oil as a cooking oil, which is a telltale sign the recipe is suspect.) The oil can be made from white or black sesame seeds. Asian sesame

DRIED LOTUS LEAF

DRIED
RED CHILI
PEPPERS

CHINESE DRIED RED DATES
(JUJUBES)

CHINESE CHILI POWDER

MUNG BEANS

DRIED LILY
FLOWERS

SICHUAN PEPPERCORNS

WHITE PEPPER
POWDER

DRIED RED CHILI PEPPERS

oils tend to be made from toasted sesame seeds, which yields the amber color. If you don't cook much Chinese food, then buy the smallest bottle of sesame oil.

SESAME PASTE: Sesame paste is made from toasted hulled sesame seeds and oil. It's not unlike peanut butter or other nut/seed butters. It's different from tahini in flavor and texture. Sesame paste is used to make dressings or sauces. You can get store-bought sesame paste in jars, or you can make your own. Toast 1 cup white sesame seeds in a large dry skillet over low heat for five to ten minutes, or until the aroma becomes warm and nutty. Let cool, then add sesame seeds to the food processor and pulse until crushed. While the processor is running, pour in 1 cup vegetable oil in a steady stream, and process until smooth. Store in an airtight container.

*SICHUAN PEPPERCORNS: These reddish-brown peppercorns are called prickly ash and are essential in Sichuan recipes. The peppercorns are fragrant and cause a tingling sensation on your tongue, especially when combined with chili sauce or hot oil. There is no substitute for Sichuan peppercorn. If you can't get to an Asian market, visit a spice shop or the bulk spice section at your market. The best Sichuan peppercorns come from Hanyuan, which you can buy online from Mala Market at TheMalaMarket.com. Before using, toast the peppercorns in a dry skillet over medium heat for 3 to 4 minutes, stirring frequently. Then grind to your preferred coarseness.

SPRING ROLL WRAPPERS: Crepe-like and square, these wrappers are used for making crispy spring rolls. They are sold frozen and are not to be confused with the Vietnamese-style round spring roll wrappers, which are dried. Wei-Chuan and Spring Home brands are widely available. Egg roll wrappers are thicker and have a different texture. When fried, egg roll wrappers become bubbly. You will have to defrost spring roll wrappers overnight in the refrigerator before using, so plan accordingly.

*SOY SAUCE: See An Ode to Soy Sauce (page 43).

*VEGETABLE OIL: A generic vegetable, soybean, canola, or neutral-flavored oil works well for cooking. Oils that have strong, distinctive flavors—such as coconut oil or olive oil—can clash with Chinese flavor profiles. The oil you use is to your preference. For my cooking, I prefer a neutral-tasting vegetable oil. A note on peanut oil: It's common to see Chinese recipes call for peanut oil. Part of that has to do with flavor and part of that has to do with the fact that peanuts are a major crop in China. Peanut-oil production is part of the economy. I don't use peanut oil because I have relatives who are allergic to nuts.

*VINEGAR: Rice vinegar, black vinegar, and distilled white vinegar all have roles in Chinese cooking. If you prefer a milder vinegar, stick with the rice vinegar. I use an unseasoned rice vinegar. If you can handle more intensity, try a Chinese black vinegar such as Chinkiang black vinegar. In a pinch, you can use an everyday balsamic vinegar—though it will add sweetness.

*WHITE PEPPER POWDER: White pepper is aged and fermented, which gives it a floral, nuanced heat. It is generally not interchangeable with black pepper. While you can buy white peppercorns and grind them yourself, it's more convenient to buy a small bottle of white pepper powder from an Asian market. You want the white pepper to lightly dust the surface of the food. You don't want to see specks of pepper.

Fresh Vegetables and Other Perishable Ingredients

This list of produce will take you through the recipes in this book. Of course, there are more vegetables and fresh items than are listed here. If your market has something in stock that looks particularly fresh and succulent, then use it in the recipe. There are few combinations in the recipes that follow that are sacred. The Chinese prefer to cook based on what's freshest and tastes the best in a given moment. If you shop at a farmers' market and a farmer is growing an interesting variety of a vegetable, then give it a try. You may discover a great combination that I wouldn't necessarily have thought of.

ASPARAGUS: Asparagus are best when they're in season in the spring, but they are available year-round. Choose slender stalks that look succulent. If the asparagus are particularly large, just be sure to cut or chop them up as necessary. **To trim:** Carefully bend the stalk and it will naturally break where the tender bit ends. Alternatively, if it seems like a waste to break off so much of the asparagus, you can simply cut about one-and-a-half inches off the bottom.

BABY BOK CHOY: Also called Shanghai bok choy, these jade-colored cabbages are widely available, even in non-Asian markets. Look for small to medium heads for the most tender leaves. The white bok choy with dark-green, dimpled leaves are heartier and may need a slightly longer cooking time. **To trim:** Slice off about a quarter inch of the core end, where sometimes there is a tiny stump. Then, snap each leaf stem as

KOREAN RADISH

EGGPLANT

GINGER

GARLIC

CILANTRO

CHINESE RADISH

YAM LEAF

BAMBOO SHOOTS

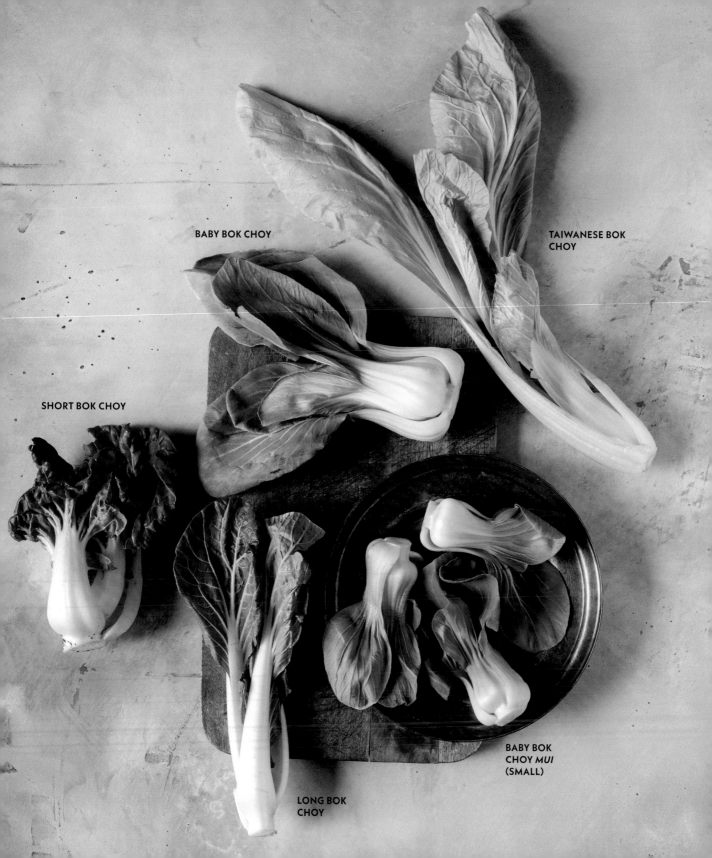

BABY BOK CHOY

TAIWANESE BOK CHOY

SHORT BOK CHOY

BABY BOK CHOY *MUI* (SMALL)

LONG BOK CHOY

close to the core as you can. Proceed with rinsing. Alternatively, slice the head of bok choy in half lengthwise. Then, cut out the core by making angled cuts on each side of the core. Remove the wedge of core. The leaves then can be separated and washed. Smaller heads of baby bok choy can be cooked whole, which looks beautiful but is hard to eat.

BAMBOO SHOOTS: It's difficult to get fresh bamboo shoots in the United States. When I've seen fresh shoots, they're really small or are starting to degrade. They resemble artichokes in how you have to shed seemingly endless layers of husk before you reach the edible part of the shoot. Canned bamboo shoots, which don't have the delicateness of fresh ones, are more commonly available. Rinse canned bamboo shoots in cold water to wash away some of that tinned flavor. In some Asian markets, you'll find boiled bamboo shoots sold in bulk. They are usually available in different forms: round, fin-shaped shoots; sliced; strips or chunks; or long, slender shoots. Include bamboo shoots in soups, stir-fries, or fillings for dumplings or buns.

BEAN SPROUTS: Bean sprouts are typically widely available—though, oddly enough, my nearby Whole Foods doesn't sell bean sprouts by choice. Wherever you buy bean sprouts, get the freshest-looking ones and check the sell-by date. If there is any sign of slime at the bottom of the package or the sprouts look brown from bruising, don't buy it. The Chinese typically add bean sprouts to cooked dishes, including soups, stir-fries, and fillings. Bean sprouts are a component of vegetable broths and add a mild flavor.

BOK CHOY: While baby bok choy (or Shanghai bok choy) has crossed into the mainstream, other varieties are slightly more obscure. Full-size bok choy have long, white stems and dark-green leaves. There is also a baby version of this variety. The texture isn't as tender as the Shanghai bok choy and requires an extra minute or two to cook.

BROCCOLI: Broccoli crowns are convenient, but don't shy away from buying whole broccoli. You can peel the stems and slice thinly to include in stir-fries. The stems also can be pickled or added to a salad. Broccolini can be used in the same way.

BRUSSELS SPROUTS: Brussels sprouts can be used in any number of stir-fry dishes that include cabbage. In the fall, farmers' markets and some grocery stores will sell whole branches of Brussels sprouts. It's a dramatic way to bring home some Brussels, but you know they're the freshest they can be. Be careful cutting them off the branch, though. The Dry-Fried Brussels Sprouts (page 144) is one of my favorite discoveries. Try anytime or at your next Thanksgiving.

BUTTERNUT SQUASH: Frozen butternut squash is a handy item to have in case you want to throw together a filling for dumplings or wontons. Blanch or steam and then mash them. Avoid pureeing the squash for a filling because it can get too runny.

CARROTS: Carrots are a staple ingredient across so many cuisines. Chinese cooking is no different. Carrots add color and texture to any stir-fry, soup, or steamed dish. Feel free to use rainbow carrots, if you are so inclined.

CAULIFLOWER: Cauliflower is great in stir-fries or steamed with aromatics. Any color of cauliflower will work fine. Be sure to cut the cauliflower in small florets to ensure even cooking but not so small that they disintegrate. Some supermarkets now sell cauliflower rice as a convenience product. Feel free to incorporate cauliflower rice, if it makes sense. Broccoflower can be treated the same way.

CELERY: Celery doesn't get enough appreciation. When thinly sliced, celery can be a star ingredient in a stir-fry. The lighter-green celery hearts are especially delicious. You can eat the leaves, too. If you can get to an Asian market, you can try Chinese celery, which has long, slender ribs and a pungent flavor. Because the heads are so slender, Chinese celery are sold in clusters. They will need to be thoroughly rinsed in cool water because they get muddy from being displayed upright, with the root end sitting in a shallow tray of water. It helps to keep the celery hydrated, but it turns the dirt into mud. Either type of celery works well for any of the recipes in this book.

CHILI PEPPERS: Use the variety of pepper that suits your level of spice tolerance. But jalapeño, Thai bird, Fresno, Korean green, and serrano are a few types of pepper that are widely available and that work well for stir-fries. Even the mostly mild shishito peppers can add wonderful flavor to a dish. Feel free to experiment with different types of peppers. Some dishes are intentionally excessive with spiciness. But I generally try not to make dishes that are off-the-charts spicy because it obliterates your ability to taste anything else.

CHINESE BROCCOLI (GAI LAN): Chinese broccoli, or *gai lan*, has dark-green leaves and long, thin or medium stalks. You can slice the stalks thinly and cook with the leaves. If you go to an Asian market, you will also find baby *gai lan* (called *gai lan mui*). These are more tender and worth the effort to seek out the next time you go to an

Asian market. While there isn't a specific recipe in this book for it, grilled *gai lan* is wonderful. **To trim:** Cut off about a half inch of the bottom of the stalks. You can leave the stalk whole, which makes them hard to eat without a fork and knife. Or you can slice the stalk thinly and roughly chop the leaves.

CHINESE CABBAGE/NAPA CABBAGE: Chinese cabbage, also called napa cabbage, is a versatile ingredient that can just as easily be a "filler" ingredient or a star. Mildly sweet, Chinese cabbage can be stir-fried, steamed, added to soups and fillings, and even used as the liner for a steamer basket full of dumplings. If you use cabbage leaves for steaming, cut the leaves in half crosswise and use the frilly part. Place the leaves in the steamer, overlapping as needed. Then arrange dumplings on top. A head of Chinese cabbage sometimes can be quite large, but it can be stored in the produce bin for a long time. There are different varieties, including long napa cabbage, which is a narrow and long cousin to regular napa. **To trim:** Peel off any outer leaves that are damaged or wilting. Cut the cabbage in half lengthwise and then cut each half into quarters. You can cut the wedge of core off and use what leaves you need and store the rest.

CHINESE EGGPLANT: Chinese and Japanese eggplants are long and thin, and range in color from dark to bright purple. Choose eggplants that are firm and don't have bruises. If you don't have access to Chinese eggplant, you can use regular eggplant—just shave off the peel before using. To trim Chinese eggplant, rinse it first. You don't need to peel it, but do cut off the green stem.

CHINESE MUSTARD GREENS (GAI CHOY): Chinese mustard greens, or *gai choy*, have a bright but pungent flavor. The larger heads have bulbous stems and unwieldy leaves. Smaller heads, often sold in multiples, are more delicate. Look for the small mustard greens in Chinese markets, where they're often labeled *xue li hong*. **To trim:** Cut about a quarter to a half inch off the core end. Then snap apart the leaves, which sometimes can be unwieldy. Rinse in cool water thoroughly before using.

CHINESE RED SPINACH: Also called *zen choy* or amaranth greens, this spinach has green and purplish-red leaves. **To trim:** Separate the leaves from the tough center stem and cook just the tender pieces.

CILANTRO: Cilantro is called *xiang cai*, or "fragrant vegetable." This herb shows up as a finishing touch in many cold and hot dishes. It adds its namesake fragrance to

GAI CHOY (CHINESE MUSTARD GREENS)

SMALL GAI CHOY

GAI LAN (CHINESE BROCCOLI)

GAI LAN MUI (BABY GAI LAN)

CHINESE CABBAGE (NAPA CABBAGE)

LONG NAPA CABBAGE

balance heavy flavors. **To trim:** You can cut off the root end. Use the leaves and the stems, which can be minced.

CORN: Fresh or frozen corn is an easy ingredient that can add sweetness to a dish. Keep a bag of corn kernels in the freezer for a back-pocket stir-fry or soup, such as Sweet Corn Soup (page 123). And if you have the first *Chinese Soul Food* book, be sure to try the Wok-Seared Corn.

CUCUMBER: In addition to being pickled, cucumber can be stir-fried or steamed. This might be unusual to the Western palate, since cucumbers tend to be served raw and in salads. The delicate green flavor is quite nice for stir-frying or steaming. For best results, use smaller, thin-skinned cucumbers such as the Persian or Japanese varieties. If you use a regular cucumber, you will have to peel it first. **To trim:** Cut off the very ends and slice as needed.

DAIKON: Daikon radish can be pickled, braised, stir-fried, steamed, or cooked in soup. Daikon tend to be long and lean, and are often sold next to Korean radish, which is rounder and squatter with a halo of green skin. While daikon is known to be milder, both types of radish will work in recipes. **To trim:** Cut off the top and tail and peel as you would a carrot.

EDAMAME: The Chinese call edamame *mao dou*, or "fuzzy bean." The shelled beans are widely available in the freezer section and can be stir-fried or steamed. When you buy edamame, do a quality check. They often are sold in clear packages or packages that have a small see-through window. Be sure the beans don't have freezer burn.

GARLIC: Look for bulbs of garlic that have bright skins and firm cloves. Avoid ones that have brown spots, feel soft, or have green sprouts in the middle. For many recipes in this book, you can finely mince, crush, or smash the garlic as specified.

GINGER: Ginger plays many flavor roles. It adds warmth and spice, but it also counterbalances any off flavors and brightens a dish. When buying, don't hesitate to look through the pile to find a succulent piece that has bright skin. If the skin is dull and wrinkly, skip it. If the piece is too large, break off the chunk that you need. The general rules for ginger in this book: There is no need to peel the ginger when the recipe calls for slices. However, peel the ginger if the recipe calls for grated or minced ginger.

GREEN ONIONS: Also known as scallions, green onions often are combined with ginger and garlic to increase the pungency of dishes. For the recipes in this book, use both the white and green parts of the stalk. If the stalks are wide (a half inch or more), make a cut down the center of the stalk lengthwise. This extra step helps prevent those large pieces that can be unpleasant to bite into. **To trim:** Cut off the root end. If any of the greens have any brown edges, trim them off.

MUSHROOMS (FRESH): The varieties of fresh mushrooms that are now available in supermarkets keep growing. Try mixing a few different kinds, such as white or brown beech mushrooms, oyster mushrooms, maitake, enoki, or whatever you might discover on your next trip to the store. If you prefer mild mushrooms, you can use the ubiquitous cremini. Should you want to splurge, you can get morels to use in a stir-fry. Put them to the flavor test in Savory Mushrooms with Rice Powder (page 159).

PEA SHOOTS: The labeling for pea shoots/sprouts and pea vines sometimes can get confusing. Bottom line is that they all taste delicious, especially when stir-fried with a hint of garlic. Not all pea shoots are equally tender, however, and it can be hit-or-miss. Micro pea shoots, usually grown by local farmers, can be particularly fresh tasting. But you'll pay a premium at four to six dollars of peas (or more) per clamshell box. A mound of sprouts will cook down to a fraction of its original volume, though. Pea vines, the leaves and tendrils from the pea plant, can get fibrous. You can mitigate that by cutting the pea vines in half or thirds across the stem.

GARLIC AND GINGER IN JARS

People ask my opinion on minced garlic or ginger in jars or tubes. I never want to intentionally create barriers for people to cook. So my response to the question about these jarred products is that if it helps you get in the kitchen, then go for it. I personally prefer fresh, unprocessed garlic and ginger because the packaged varieties have to have some sort of preservation process or ingredients that may or may not be natural to keep the garlic and ginger from turning. As an example, these are the ingredients listed on a tube of garlic paste: garlic, canola oil, whey (milk) sodium lactate, sea salt, dextrose, glycerin, citric acid, calcium chloride, and xanthan gum. That's more than I want in my garlic. Also, once processed and packaged, the garlic and ginger intensify in flavor, which is not always a good thing. If the flavors are too strong, then it could throw off the balance of a dish.

PEAS: Frozen green peas are a staple that can add flavor and color to a dish. You likely already keep frozen peas in the freezer for other purposes. It doesn't hurt to keep an extra bag of peas so you can add a handful to a dish when desired. Peas don't take much time to defrost when you throw them into a stir-fry, but you can help them along by placing the peas in a bowl of hot water from the faucet. Drain before tossing the peas into the dish you're cooking.

SHALLOTS: Fresh shallots aren't as commonly used in Chinese recipes as green onions, but you need them if you're going to make your own fried shallots (page 132), which do get used as a crunchy topping. Look for bulbs that are firm and have bright skin. The Chili-Shallot Jam (page 174) that accompanies steamed sweet potatoes is also excellent for any number of applications, where a sweet-oniony flavor would be complementary.

SNOW PEAS: Snow peas appear in recipes as much for a pop of color as for texture and flavor. Select bright green snow peas that don't have brown spots or wrinkled skin. Keeping them whole makes sense for most preparations. You can also can slice them on the bias for a different effect. **To trim:** Snap off the stem before using.

SOY MILK: Soy milk is made from soybeans and comes sweetened and unsweetened. Soy milk is widely available and also comes in flavors. In the context of this book, straight-up, traditional soy milk is featured in a breakfast recipe that treats the milk like a savory soup (page 218), topped with pickles and served with *youtiao* (Chinese crullers).

SWEET BELL PEPPERS: Sweet bell peppers can brighten a dish, but they can be expensive. I like buying the bags of mini sweet peppers so that I can get red, orange, and yellow colors. Regular sweet bell peppers can be quite large and yield more than a recipe needs. It's nice to have smaller peppers so you potentially waste less.

TAIWANESE CABBAGE: Taiwanese cabbage looks like supersized, flattened green cabbage. It has a mildly sweet flavor and doesn't need much more than a few minutes in a hot wok with a dash of soy sauce. When buying, look for the smallest head you think you could reasonably consume in a few weeks. Asian markets often cut the larger cabbages into halves. Before cooking Taiwanese cabbage, I like to salt the leaves by adding a pinch of salt and squeezing handfuls of cabbage leaves to work it in. This is how we begin to build flavor and make the leaves easier to cook. **To trim:** Remove any damaged outer leaves. Cut out the hard inner core.

YU CHOY

TAGU CHOY

TONG HO (CHRYSANTHEMUM GREENS)

AMARANTH GREENS

TAIWANESE CABBAGE

CHINESE CELERY

PEA VINES

PEA SHOOTS

TOFU OR BEAN CURD: Tofu is made from soy milk curds that are pressed into blocks of different firmness: soft, medium, firm, and extra-firm. Tofu is ubiquitous in Chinese cooking, appearing in every form in every type of dish from appetizers to desserts. Japanese silken tofu, which is sold in aseptic boxes, is not pressed like Chinese tofu is. Silken tofu is smooth and extremely delicate in texture. For the purposes of the stir-fries and soups in this book, I prefer Chinese-style soft or medium-firm tofu.

TOFU GAN: Also called spiced tofu, five-spice tofu, or pressed tofu, this tofu is seasoned with five-spice flavors and becomes extra-firm after pressing. It's usually used in cold salads or stir-fries. Typically, it comes packaged in small square slabs that you can slice or julienne.

TOFU PUFFS: These are puffy fried cubes of tofu that can be added to stir-fries or soups. For the Kung Pao Tofu Puffs (page 199), you can use store-bought or homemade tofu puffs.

TOFU OR BEAN CURD SKIN OR SHEETS: The nomenclature is confusing because tofu sheets can describe a range of products that are all made of bean curd and sold in sheet form. But there are key differences. Tofu skin, also called yuba, is made of the skin that forms on the surface of soy milk and is dried in flat pieces or as rolled-up sticks. It is usually added to soups or stir-fries. There is also a version of tofu skin that is dried but still pliable. These sheets are found in the refrigerated section and are used as wrappers for steamed or fried tofu rolls. Finally, there are bean curd sheets that are essentially tofu that's been pressed into one-eighth-inch-thick squares. These can be cut into tofu noodles, which you can use in cold salads or stir-fries.

TOMATOES: While summer tomatoes taste the best, winter tomatoes can hold their own when incorporated in a stir-fry, soup, or Dad's Steamed Eggs with Tomatoes (page 228). Varieties such as Roma and the generic "hot house tomatoes" are fine. I also have found that cherry tomatoes are relatively consistent in flavor. It's not necessary to peel the tomatoes.

WINTER MELON (GOURD): Winter melon resembles watermelon in shape. Whether oblong or round, winter melon can have a thick rind that ranges in color from solid deep green to light green with creamy striations. The flesh is white and turns translucent when cooked or candied. It pairs well with smoky flavors. Winter melon is typically sold in chunks. Fair warning: Some varieties may have very stringy, spaghetti squash-like flesh. That may be a shock if you're used to eating the tender variety. **To trim:** If you have a whole winter melon, you will need to cut it into smaller wedges first. Scrape out the seeds and, using a knife, carefully shave off the rind before cooking. The rind can be quite hard, so be careful.

WONTON WRAPPERS: Wonton wrappers (square) are widely available in many supermarkets. If you can get to a Chinese market, you will be able to find different thicknesses of wonton wrappers. The packages will denote the specific usage: Where a thin wrapper might be used for wonton soup, a thicker wrapper might be used for fried wontons. You can keep a pack or two in the freezer and defrost as needed.

YAM LEAF: Asian markets sell yam leaves in large bags. You have to separate the leaves from the fibrous stems. The leaves have an earthy flavor. Stir-frying with a little garlic is an easy way to enjoy yam leaf. A giant pile of leaves will cook down to a fraction of itself. From a flavor perspective, a little goes a long way. **To trim:** Pluck the tender leaves off the fibrous central stem. Cook the leaves.

YU CHOY: Yu choy is otherwise known as rapeseed, which is the plant from which oil is derived. Look for a bunch with unbruised leaves. Asian markets sell baby yu choy, which is more tender than its mature counterpart. Stir-frying is the go-to option for cooking yu choy. **To trim:** Cut off about a half inch of the end. The rest of the central stem and the leaves can be sliced or roughly chopped.

An Ode to Soy Sauce

It's no secret that my soapbox is actually a five-gallon bucket of soy sauce. Someday, maybe I'll write a soy sauce bible. In the meantime, I am determined to encourage as many people as I can to explore the vast world of soy sauces.

When I teach one of my Chinese cooking classes, I always ground the students first in a mini lecture on soy sauce. When I ask whether anyone has a bottle of Kikkoman at home, almost all the students raise their hands. Kikkoman is a perfectly fine brand of soy sauce that's globally available and serves it purpose. But most people don't go through life drinking just one kind of wine, beer, coffee, soda, or even water. We don't eat just one kind of cheese or chips or any number of foods. Have you ever gotten into a debate about which potato chips are the best? I certainly have. Why then wouldn't you try different types of soy sauce? You still may prefer the Kikkoman, but at least you'll have an inkling about the diversity of flavors that exist in soy sauce.

In the context of this book on vegetable cooking, soy sauce's role is critical. Where a vegetable dish might normally have a hint of small dried shrimp, minced beef, or chicken broth as a flavor component, a vegetarian dish must build dimension in other ways. Mushrooms, pickles, aromatics, and such are obvious pairings. Soy sauce, for many dishes, is what provides savoriness—it's not just a salty flavor. A good way to test this for yourself is to stir-fry some baby bok choy with two different soy sauces. The results can be eye-opening.

Just like any other product, the flavor profiles of soy sauces are different across makers, regions, countries, and cultures. The type of soybeans, how they're brewed and fermented, how long they're aged, and whether there are additional seasonings all contribute to how the soy sauce tastes. From Asian cuisine to Asian cuisine, the general flavor profiles of soy sauces differ and so do their uses. An all-purpose Chinese soy sauce that you use for high-heat stir-frying is not the same kind of aged Japanese shoyu that might be served with a pristine piece of sushi. Between just those two examples lies an astonishing diversity of soy sauces.

As an exercise, a friend who's a certified sommelier and I tasted Kikkoman and ten Chinese brands of soy sauces. The one anomaly is the Wan Ja Shan "tamari soy sauce," which is produced in New York State. I poured samples into Riedel wine glasses so we could sniff the aroma of each and taste. Then I added each to a hot wok to mimic stir-frying and tasted the sauces cooked. Our notes follow:

Brand	Type	Ingredient details	Country of origin	Sodium mg per 1 Tbsp.	Sodium (%)	Aroma	Flavor (raw)	Flavor (cooked)
Kikkoman	All-purpose	Water, wheat, soybeans, salt, sodium benzoate	Japan	920	38	Light caramel, dried herbs, cardboard, lightly sweet	Salt-forward, lightly toasted, lacks complexity	Salty flavors intensified, becomes better with reduction
Kimlan	All-purpose	Water, soybeans, wheat, salt, sugar	Taiwan	744	31	Caramel, molasses, nutty, briny	Salty with caramel and fruity finish	Flavors round out, with more meaty notes
Kimlan	Lower-sodium	Water, soybeans, wheat, salt, sugar, seasoning agents, licorice abstract; non-GMO	Taiwan	505	21	Rich caramel, sassafras, hint of woodiness	Slightly sweet, fruity, finishes with umami savoriness	Fruity, consommé-like, slight sweetness
Kimlan	Chinese label	Water, salt, soybeans, wheat, sugar	Taiwan	744	31	Musty, woody, briny, slightly herbal	Intense flavor, rich, salty, fruity	Intensifies salt, throws off balance
Ta-Tung Phoenix Black Bean Soy Sauce	Black bean	Black beans, water, sugar, salt, yeast extract	Taiwan	423	20	Toasted nuts, caramel, brown sugar, spice, black pepper, floral, dark fruit	Sweet, molasses, fermented	Caramel intensifies, rich, broth-like, complex finish, fruity
Wei-Chuan	Premium, gold label	Water, sugar, soybeans, wheat, salt, alcohol, yeast powder	Taiwan	740	31	Earthy, blanched almond, fruity, raw mushroom, meaty	Savory and rich, coats palate, fruity, integrated salt, rounded	Intensifies rich flavor, caramelized vegetables, long finish

Brand	Type	Ingredient details	Country of origin	Sodium mg per 1 Tbsp.	Sodium (%)	Aroma	Flavor (raw)	Flavor (cooked)
Wuan Chuang	n/a	Black beans, salt, sugar, soybeans, wheat, seasoning agents (yeast extract, disodium succinate), sweetening agents (trisodium glycyrrhizinate)	Taiwan	819	34	Cedar, earthy, mushroom, potting soil, gamey, umami	Tastes like it smells, musty	Sweetness, gamey, salty
O'Long	Premium black bean	Water, black soybean extract, salt, sugar	Taiwan	868	36	Dark caramel, dried mushroom, forest floor	Maple syrup, baking spice, briny, sweet-salt	Sweet-salt intensifies, integrates flavors
Lee Kum Kee	Premium dark	Water, salt, caramel color, sugar, soybeans, wheat	China	1,180	49	Rich caramel, molasses, spice, woody, fruit	Light molasses, salty, strong, overpowering	Intensely salty, toasted nuts, long finish, mustiness intensifies
Koon Chun	Thick	Molasses, water, sugar, salt, soy sauce	Hong Kong	540	23	Molasses, cinnamon	Burnt molasses, baking spice, bitter finish	Bitter, unpleasant
Wan Ja Shan	Organic gluten-free tamari	Water, organic whole soybeans, salt, organic evaporated cane juice	USA	910	38	Ale-like, fermentation, green herb, astringent, floral	Salty, yeasty, resinous herb on finish	Salt intensifies, slight fruitiness

You can see from the tasting notes some of our impressions. This chart doesn't even begin to cover the options of soy sauces available at any major Chinese supermarket. The point here isn't to rank the soy sauces because which one is best is purely personal. That said, the Wei-Chuan gold label soy sauce has consistently won awards for flavor.

Every Chinese person has a favorite brand of soy sauce, or they "inherit" a preference for a given brand because that's simply what they grew up eating. I grew up with Wei-Chuan all-purpose soy sauce from Taiwan. Wei-Chuan is a trusted food company that makes many different products. In my family's Chinese restaurant in the 1980s and 1990s in Columbia, Missouri, having access to a trusted Chinese brand for wholesale soy sauce was a big deal. After I graduated college and left home to make my way in the newspaper business, being able to find Wei-Chuan soy sauce in my new home in Denver, Colorado, was also a way for me to stay connected with the flavors of home. Sadly, after I moved to Seattle, the Wei-Chuan soy sauce that I grew up with was discontinued. I had to find a new favorite. After trying a few, I eventually landed on an all-purpose Kimlan soy sauce with the yellow and red label. I do love the Wei-Chuan gold label, but it's not easy to find in the United States.

Over time, especially in the last few years, the number of soy sauces that have become available is staggering. As I'm writing this, I can think of the number of high-end soy sauces that have hit the shelves in the past year. This is a change in culture. Previously, most bottles of Chinese soy sauces hovered in the three to five dollars range. Now, there are several soy sauces, packed in beautiful boxes, that range from fifteen to thirty dollars. This is remarkable because the Chinese don't typically like spending that much money for soy sauce.

A few reminders for how to buy soy sauce:
- Look for a soy sauce that is naturally brewed and fermented. It will say this on the label. This means the soy sauce was produced in the proper way and not with chemical short-cuts—i.e., hydrolyzed soy protein. It's the difference between real maple syrup versus corn syrup with maple flavoring.
- Light soy sauce refers to the color and viscosity, not calorie count.
- Dark soy sauce is often used for braising.
- Aged soy sauce tends to have intense flavors.
- Low-sodium soy sauce still has plenty of sodium, so be aware if you have to watch your sodium intake.
- Tamari is a Japanese-style soy sauce that is usually, but not always, wheat-free. Check the label to be sure.
- There is no substitute for soy sauce. Aminos mimic the flavor, but they're just not the same and some brands actually have an off-putting taste. Coconut aminos are too sweet for savory dishes, though they're fine for dipping sauces.

Equipment

Chinese cooking tools are relatively inexpensive. We emphasize the cachet of ingredients versus the "braggability" of the cookware. A traditional wok, steamer, cleaver, wok spatula, and such are generally affordable. If you've spent more than forty or fifty dollars on a 12-inch wok, you've spent too much. An expensive cleaver might be forty dollars. High-end cookware brands have delved into making tools for Chinese cooking, resulting in woks that are one hundred to three hundred dollars and made in nontraditional materials that don't align with wok-cooking techniques. It's the same with wok spatulas. I always end up getting the seven dollars any-Chinese-brand wok spatula that has a thin blade and a handle that is angled appropriately for proper stir-fry technique.

The following list of equipment includes items that I use in my cross-cultural kitchen.

CANNING JARS: Canning jars are useful for pickling and fermenting, as well as storing spices and condiments, such as Chili-Shallot Jam (page 174). Have a selection of sizes, including half-pint-, pint-, and quart-size jars. While there aren't any canned recipes in this book, there are a few ferments, so be sure to buy appropriate lids and rings to pair with the specific style of jar.

CHEF'S KNIFE: An eight-inch chef's knife is worth investing in. This is the knife that will get you through most tasks. What brand you buy is a personal choice that depends on budget and how a knife feels in your hand. The material used to make the knife determines its weight and balance. Visit a reputable knife shop or kitchenware shop to try different knives. Personally, I prefer a Japanese-style chef's knife, which tends to be lighter and balanced just right for my smaller hands.

CHOPSTICKS: You eat with chopsticks, but you can also cook with chopsticks. Chopsticks can be used for a range of tasks in the kitchen, including beating eggs, mixing fillings for dumplings, filling dumplings, frying foods, and placing or arranging foods on plates. Everyday bamboo chopsticks are great, or you can buy cooking chopsticks, which are about fifteen inches long. The extra length makes it easier to handle ingredients that are still in the active stages of cooking. Chopstick styles do differ from culture to culture. Where Japanese chopsticks tend to taper to a point, Chinese chopsticks tend to be thicker and have a blunt, round tip.

CLEAVER: A cleaver is a great multitasking tool. You can slice, chop, smash, crack, and use the blade like a bench scraper to scoop up ingredients. All Asian markets sell cleavers. The Chinese markets often have inexpensive cleavers that get the job done. It's not necessary to buy a high-end cleaver, unless you choose to. A thirty- to forty-dollar cleaver is perfectly fine. Look for ones with stainless carbon steel for ease of care. (Note: A cleaver intended for meat butchering will have a thicker blade. So if you are interested in buying a cleaver and you also eat meat, consider this aspect in your decision. Usually, a cook will turn the cleaver upside down to use the thicker, blunt edge to crack, say, a chicken bone and then use the sharp edge to maneuver and cut out the broken segment of bone.)

CUTTING BOARD: I have a selection of cutting boards, including small and large plastic boards, a Boos Block, and a couple of bamboo boards that came in pack of two. The wooden boards double as giant trivets. You don't need to have as many boards as I do, but I suggest having at least two.

DUTCH DOUGH MIXER: This contraption is great for mixing dough by hand. It has a wooden or metal handle much like a whisk and a looped, sturdy wire at the end that's used to combine flour and liquid. I came across one of these in a cookware shop a couple of decades ago and have had one in my kitchen ever since. This is not an imperative buy, however. You can just as easily mix dough with a spoon, a pair of chopsticks, a rubber spatula, or your hands.

FAT SKIMMER: This is a fine-mesh tool with an upright handle that is great for skimming the scum off the surface of broths or braises, or the debris from deep frying.

FINE-MESH SIEVES: I keep assorted sizes of fine-mesh sieves for straining broths or sauces that contain loose aromatics, or ingredients that require soaking.

FOOD PROCESSOR: A food processor is handy for making some fillings for steamed baozi and assorted dumplings. It's not imperative to use a food processor, but if you have one, it is efficient. Be sure to pay attention and not overprocess ingredients.

LADLE: A ladle is good for soups, of course, but it's also handy for making hot-water doughs. The style of ladle (stainless, silicone, plastic, etc.) is up to your preference. I like stainless-steel ladles with rubber grips.

MEASURING CUPS AND SPOONS: You likely already have standard measuring cups and spoons. I also love and frequently use the mini four-tablespoon angled measuring cup from OXO, which is ideal for measuring soy sauce, oil, and other liquid ingredients. Trying to measure a tablespoon of soy sauce using a measuring spoon can be an accident waiting to happen. But the mini angled measuring cup solves that problem.

METAL WORK BOWLS: I keep a stack of lightweight, stainless-steel work bowls in several sizes. They're durable, convenient, and essential for containing all the prepped ingredients. If you can find shallow metal dishes, these are great for steaming. Like the full-size work bowls, the shallow dishes come in graduated sizes. Be sure to get one or two that fit your steamer, with enough clearance to allow the steam to flow.

PICKLING JAR (CHINESE): This traditional jar has a system that allows you to use a water seal that prevents oxygen from getting inside. There's a "moat" at the neck of the shapely vaselike jar and an inverted bowl that serves as the lid. Once the lid is placed, you add water to the reservoir, refilling as needed.

RICE COOKER: Cooking rice on the stove is straightforward and some people prefer it, but I'm team rice cooker for life. Rice cookers range from the conventional one-button models that get the job done to high-end computerized cookers that are programmable and adjust the soaking, cooking, and steaming times according to the type of rice. The cost can be anywhere from twenty to five hundred dollars (see page 179). For one person, a three- or six-cup, no-frills cooker is just fine. A family is better served by a ten-cup rice cooker. For sixty to seventy dollars, you can get a decent rice cooker that has settings to cook several varieties of rice. Aficionados who are willing to drop a few hundred bucks can get a rice cooker that uses fuzzy logic technology, which, among many features, can sense if the rice is cooking too quickly and adjust the heat as necessary.

SPIDER

CHINESE
CLEAVER

JAPANESE
VEGETABLE
CLEAVER

WOK SPATULA

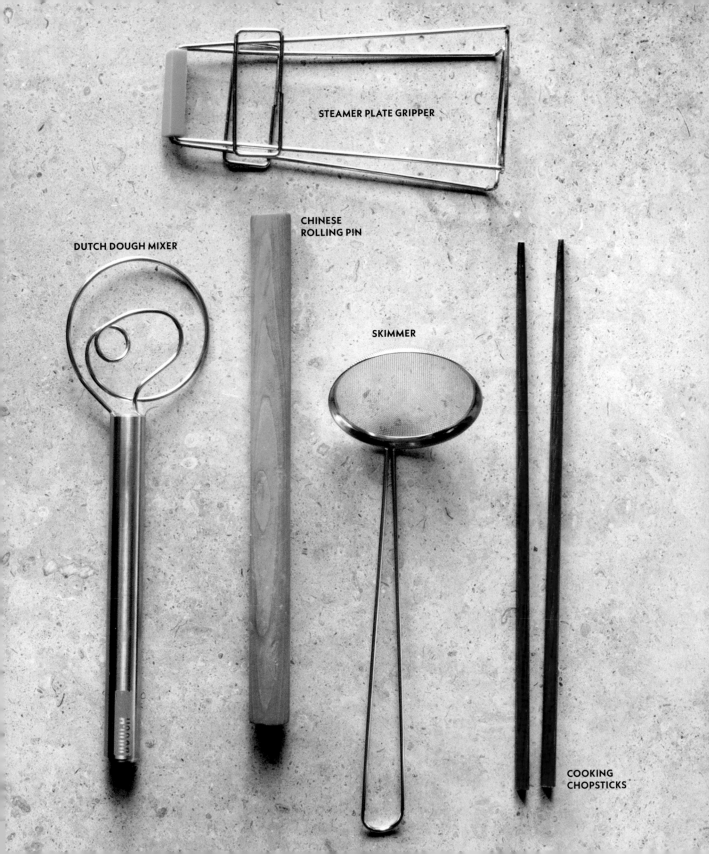

STEAMER PLATE GRIPPER

CHINESE
ROLLING PIN

DUTCH DOUGH MIXER

SKIMMER

COOKING
CHOPSTICKS

ROLLING PIN: Chinese rolling pins are glorified wooden dowels. They're typically about twelve inches long and about three-quarter inch in diameter. Some may be longer or shorter, but the pins are straight, not tapered, and are inexpensive to buy at an Asian market. Depending on the type of wood, a rolling pin will cost two to ten dollars. This is a necessary tool for making dumplings from scratch. If you do get a wooden dowel from the hardware store, be sure to get one that's made from a heavier wood and has about a three-quarter-inch diameter with a smooth surface.

SAUCE DISHES: Small ceramic sauce dishes are useful not only for dipping sauces but also for holding the spices and aromatics that will go into a recipe. Especially when stir-frying and dealing with high heat, having all of your ingredients measured, lined up, and ready to go is key to preventing overcooking and scorching. Asian markets have the largest selection of designs. (Daiso, an international Japanese discount store, sells very inexpensive sauce dishes.)

SCALE: Get a digital scale that can switch between US and metric units. Using weight is a much more accurate way to measure ingredients. About ten dollars will get you a decent food scale. You could spend more to get fancier ones. I've found that the simplest digital scales with straightforward functions work the best.

SPICE GRINDER: If you have a spice grinder, it is useful for grinding Sichuan peppercorns. This can be accomplished with a pepper mill too, if you want to get a dedicated mill. I find that using a mortar and pestle doesn't break up the peppercorns as finely as I would like—though that is likely more a reflection of my impatience to pound the peppercorns long enough to achieve the proper coarseness.

STEAMER: Steamers are available in bamboo, stainless steel, and aluminum (see photo on opposite page). You can find an assortment of dedicated steamer pots at any Asian market or online. I prefer to use bamboo because it's absorbent and prevents condensation. On metal or glass steamer lids, the condensation drips back down on your food, leaving water spots. If you have beautiful dumplings, you don't want water spots. When buying, choose a three-piece, ten-inch bamboo steamer set plus an eleven-inch steaming ring that will allow you to convert a Dutch oven or stockpot into a steamer system. If you are thinking about buying a stainless-steel steamer from a non-Chinese cookware maker, be sure the holes are big enough to allow the steam to rise. If the holes in the steamer basket are skewer size, I suggest considering a different brand/style of steamer. **Setting up a steamer:** Fill the pot with water, leaving one-and-a-half to two inches of headspace. Bring to a boil over high heat, then turn

14-INCH ALUMINUM STEAMER

10-INCH BAMBOO STEAMER

12-INCH STAINLESS
STEEL STEAMER

down the heat to medium. Set the steamer ring on the rim of the pot. Set the steamer basket containing food on the steamer ring and cover with the lid.

STEAMER HOT PLATE GRIPPER/TONGS: These special gripper tongs are for lifting hot dishes out of a steamer. I prefer the folding-style gripper versus the clip-style. They're easier to use when trying to lift a heavy plate of food out of a hot steamer.

STEAMER PAPER: You can get precut, perforated parchment circles to line your steamer. Food-safe synthetic-cotton steamer sheets are also available at some Chinese markets. This prevents food from sticking.

STRAINER/SPIDER: A spider is useful for straining and lifting foods out of hot oil or boiling water. There are many styles of spiders. You can get a traditional wire and bamboo version or something stainless steel. It's not necessary to spend too much money on a spider. I have several types that I use for different situations.

WOK: If you are committed to cooking more Chinese food, then get a wok. Look for a carbon-steel, twelve-inch wok that either has a flat bottom for flat-top stoves or a traditional round bottom for gas stoves. You should not spend more than fifty dollars on a wok. Many are priced around thirty dollars. I recently discovered the Mammafong woks produced by an Australian company and available via Amazon. These are hand-hammered and well made. I bought one for my collection and also gave some as gifts. Avoid stainless steel (food sticks, heavy) and Western-style cast-iron woks (slow to heat, retains heat too long, very heavy). Every Asian market sells woks, but you can buy them online easily. If you'd like to choose the configuration of your wok, WokShop.com offers woks with many options. You can select the size of wok, type of bottom, styles of handles, and all the necessary accessories.

WOK LADLE: A wok ladle has a long handle and a bowl-like spoon. It can be used to stir-fry and to serve soups or other hot liquids. Unlike a regular ladle, the handle of a wok ladle is level with the bowl. The restaurant-style wok ladles tend to be larger, with even longer handles. They're made to use with commercial woks and stoves. I find that those are too big for home use, though if you have a taller stature, it may be suitable. There's no need to spend more than fifteen dollars.

WOK SPATULA: A wok spatula has a long handle and a wide, thin blade that helps you scoop and toss ingredients in a wok. I prefer ones that have a thin, metal blade versus bamboo or plastic. Look for wok spatulas online or at an Asian market. You shouldn't spend more than fifteen dollars.

How to Season and Maintain a Wok

For a new wok, scrub it with soap and hot tap water to rid the surface of the factory finish. Dry with a towel. Set the wok on the stove and turn the heat to high. The heat helps to dry the wok completely. When the wok is really hot, there will be tiny wisps of smoke.

Next, coat the wok with oil: Starting from about 2 inches below the rim, slowly and in a swirling motion pour 3 tablespoons of vegetable oil down the side of the wok. Turn the heat to low. Add 1 bunch of green onions that's been cut into 3-inch segments and ½ cup of sliced ginger coins (¼ inch thick; no need to peel). It will sizzle a bit.

Using your wok spatula, stir and toss the onions and ginger together. Then, using the combination like a sponge, push it up and down the sides of the wok to help coat the surface with oil. Do this for 2 to 3 minutes. Turn off the heat, and discard the onions and ginger. Wipe the wok with a wad of paper towel to absorb any excess oil. Let cool. The wok is ready to go. Over time, especially if you use the wok to fry, the oil will help to develop the patina in the wok.

Treat a wok like a cast-iron pan. After the initial seasoning of the wok, don't use soap to wash it after use. Rinse immediately in warm water after use and give it a gentle scrub with sponge. Dry thoroughly to prevent rusting. Put it back on the stove to heat for about 1 minute to dry. If you do get some rust, scrub it with steel wool and re-season.

Techniques

Building confidence in the kitchen is not about memorizing a recipe or knowing how to cook everything. Even professional, award-winning chefs don't know how to cook *everything*. There are too many cuisines and sub-cuisines for any one person to be expert at all. Rather, confidence comes from internalizing some basic techniques in cooking, so that you don't have to think about them, and building familiarity and ease with a given recipe or type of cooking through repetition. Yes, practice makes confidence.

So, let's check our expectations. While nothing is particularly difficult to make in this book, a handful of recipes are more time-consuming and take more patience than others. To the best of my abilities, I have streamlined the methods to make them accessible to cooks of all skill levels. What follows are some general tips on building your cooking practice and some notes on how to think like a Chinese home cook.

Preparing Ingredients

What follows are some general tips on preparing dried ingredients, as well as notes for processing fresh ingredients.

Dried Ingredients

Stocking a key selection of pantry items will help you make many of the recipes in this book at any time. Dried shiitake, wood ear, bean thread, lily flowers, rice vermicelli, mung beans, and red beans are among the ingredients that require soaking for thirty minutes up to overnight. When you read the recipes in advance, you will know how much time to allow for soaking. Be sure to store dried ingredients in sealable containers or bags to maintain freshness. Some sample ingredients and their soaking times can be found on page 58.

One caveat about soaking mushrooms: There is a school of thought on saving the soaking liquid to add to the dish or soup that you are making. The idea is that the liquid has good mushroom flavor and can enhance the recipe. If you plan on using the soaking liquid, then it would be best to filter it first. You can do that by pouring it through an extra-fine sieve or cheesecloth to strain out the grit.

Good Habits

Understanding the logistics of cooking and being in the practice of thinking ahead is a challenge. Often, simply deciding what to cook is daunting enough. Believe it or not, I face that question every day with the tiniest bit of dread. What goes through my mind: What's in the fridge? What's in the pantry? Can I get home in time from my "day job" to make XYZ meal or do I have time for only a one-pot (or one-wok) meal? What are the kids' current food hang-ups and what's the least disruptive path to put dinner on the table? So, really, who has time to think about soaking mushrooms? But, soaking dried ingredients in advance is part of the logistics. If I remember to do it before I go to work, great. If I don't, I have to adapt. Whatever the situation, I don't beat myself up for it. If you're the type of person who needs permission to change course, I hereby grant you permission to skip the dried ingredient (if it's a minor component) or switch gears completely. If you're cooking at home, you're already ahead of the game.

Regardless of what cuisine you're cooking, there are some general habits worth establishing:

READ THE RECIPE: Give yourself enough time to process what you've read. If you don't have time, then you probably should make something tried-and-true and not attempt an unfamiliar recipe when you're in a rush. Reading the recipe also will prepare you for any steps in the recipe that might require extra time or advance work, such as soaking dried ingredients that need reconstituting, resting dough, or marinating.

START WITH AN UNCLUTTERED WORKSPACE: This is relative to the size of your kitchen, of course. Even if you're in a galley or a kitchenette, you still can organize the immediate space you're using and wipe down the surfaces. This is important because . . . (see next item).

MISE EN PLACE: This is the French term for "put everything in place." This is especially crucial when you are stir-frying. Once you start a stir-fry in a sizzling wok, you have seconds to add ingredients. If your ingredients aren't prepped or measured and ready to go, then something is going to burn.

CLEAN AS YOU GO: Well, try to. At least put dirty work bowls and such in or by the sink.

TAKE CARE OF YOUR TOOLS: Clean and put them away. Specifically, take care of your wok and bamboo steamer. If you use your wok, clean it right away or right after dinner. Do not let it soak for an extended period of time or you might strip away the patina. If you use your bamboo steamer, rinse/scrub off any food that has stuck to it with a clean sponge, but don't use soap. Let it air-dry before storing. Do NOT put the wok or bamboo steamer in a dishwasher.

INGREDIENT SOAKING TIME

Ingredient	Soaking time (approx.)
Dried shiitake	2 to 3 hours
Dried kelp	30 minutes
Dried wood ear	30 to 60 minutes
Dried lily flowers	20 to 30 minutes
Rice vermicelli noodles	15 to 20 minutes
Bean thread noodles	10 to 15 minutes
Red beans	Overnight
Mung beans	Overnight

Produce

To wash bunched, stalky greens, such as yu choy and *gai lan*, place them in a large bowl in the sink. Fill with cool water and swish around, making sure to gently rub off any dirt or grit that might be hiding in the nooks and crannies. It may require a couple of changes of water.

For baby bok choy, Chinese mustard greens (*gai choy*), and other similar head vegetables, separate the leaves from the core first before swishing in a large bowl of water. For Chinese cabbage, Taiwanese cabbage, and similar, trim off any outer leaves that might be wilted or bruised. There's no need to wash the interior.

If you have a bunch of greens that perhaps have been in the produce bin for a touch too long and are wilting but not yellowed and desiccated, you can soak them in a large bowl of cool water for thirty minutes to refresh them.

Cutting

BIAS CUT: Vegetables and aromatics can be sliced thinly on the bias to help create surface area and a visually appealing appearance. When you slice on the bias, the pieces shingle nicely, which makes it easy to cut julienne.

CHOP: Chopping involves cutting ingredients into smaller pieces, with approximate dimensions that usually aren't uniform. In Chinese cooking, chopping also refers to

DICE

ROLL CUT

SLICE

BIAS CUT

DICE

MINCE

SLIVER

using a cleaver to ax through a hard vegetable or rind or to use a continuous staccato motion to transform larger chunks into a mince.

DICE: Dice can range from tiny (one-eighth inch) to large (three-quarter inch), depending on the type of vegetable and preparation. Cut into strips first and then cluster the strips and cut them crosswise into the desired size.

MINCE: Mincing, in this book, is used mainly for aromatics, such as garlic and ginger. You can also use a garlic press for cloves of garlic and a Microplane-type zester to grate fresh ginger. To remove the garlic skin, place the clove on a cutting board. Place the flat side of your knife blade on top of the clove. Place the palm of your other hand on the knife blade above the garlic clove. Press down firmly to smash the garlic clove. The skin will peel off easily. Alternatively, you can use the flat side of a cleaver and firmly smack the clove of garlic. To peel ginger, you can use a vegetable peeler, a sharp knife, or a spoon to scrape off the skin.

SLICE: Slices yield thinly cut rounds of ginger, carrots, cucumber, and the like.

SLIVERS (JULIENNE): Fine, threadlike cuts of aromatics and vegetables, slivers are commonly used for garnishes or for hard vegetables, such as carrots, so that they cook more quickly.

Combining Ingredients

The beauty of most of the recipes in this book is that the ingredients are interchangeable. If a recipe works with one type of leafy green vegetable, it will work with other similar leafy green vegetables. The same goes for sauces. The goal for any dish is to balance flavors and textures. If something is salty/savory, you may desire to add a hint of sweetness to tone it down. For a contrast, you may add a touch of vinegar to brighten the flavor. Perhaps you like spice. You could add a fiery chili sauce or just a pinch of white pepper powder. A drizzle of sesame oil at the end of a stir-fry adds a toasty nuttiness to the flavor. After you've tried a few dishes and discovered combinations you like, feel free to play with the combinations and layering of flavors. What follows is a guide with a loose formula for how you might create combinations.

Think about what cooking method you're using, then choose a main ingredient, such as baby bok choy. Decide what secondary ingredients sound good to you, then choose flavors from the remaining columns. This is not the order that you add the ingredients; it's meant to be a visual tool to help you conceptualize a dish.

Example:
- Baby bok choy + shiitake, carrots, snow peas + ginger, garlic, green onions, white pepper powder + rice wine + soy sauce + sesame oil, vegetable oil.
- Baby bok choy + wood ear, bean sprouts + pickles + soy sauce + sugar + vegetable oil, sesame oil.
- Eggplant + sweet bell peppers + ginger, garlic, leeks + rice wine, vinegar + soy sauce, fermented black beans + sugar + vegetable oil, chili oil.

The following chart is not comprehensive, but it should give you a starting point for how to orient your thinking around combining ingredients and flavors.

Main ingredient	Paired with	Spice/ aromatics	Acid	Salty/ savory	Sweet	Fat (cooking and finishing)
Asparagus	Shiitake	Ginger	Rice wine	Soy sauce or salt	Sugar	Sesame oil
Baby bok choy	Bean sprouts	Garlic	Vinegar	Pickles	Dried red dates	Chili oil
Brussels sprouts	Carrots	Green onion, leek, or shallots	Pickles	Fermented black beans		Vegetable oil
Chinese cabbage	Celery	Chili	Citrus	Seaweed		
Gai lan	Wood ear	Sichuan peppercorns		Hoisin sauce		
Chinese eggplant	Sweet bell peppers	White pepper powder	Vinegar	Soy sauce	Sugar	Sesame oil
Tofu	Snow peas	Green onions, garlic		Salt		Vegetable oil

Mastering Heat

Every stove is different and so is your particular set of cookware. Thus, a recipe can only provide guidelines when it comes to temperature and timing. The medium on my high-powered gas stove is certainly hotter than the medium on an average apartment electric range. What you have to do is learn the idiosyncrasies of your setup. If you don't have a high-powered stove, then you know it will take longer to preheat your wok and the cooking times will be longer too.

If you do have a high-end stove, with high BTUs or a stand-alone wok burner, you may have to shorten the cooking times. For comparison, an average home gas stove may have 12,000 to 15,000 BTUs. A high-end stove may have 23,000 BTUs. The wok stoves in restaurants may have 150,000 BTUs. The difference is extreme. It's also why it's difficult to replicate the *guo chi* or *wok hay*—the telltale seared flavor that comes from high heat and carbon steel—that you get in a proper Chinese restaurant. The most straightforward way to mitigate that advantage in your home kitchen is to not overcrowd your wok.

It should be visibly and audibly apparent if your food is cooking too fast or too slow. If the ingredients hit the wok and the immediate sizzle dies instantaneously, you've likely added too much food. Learning how to adjust the heat and/or timing is part of the cooking process, though. Like any other skill, it's a sensibility you develop over time. I certainly don't count myself as a master. I am *mastering*, and I am well versed in my particular kitchen setup, but I'm not a master. So, again, be kind to yourself as you learn.

Factors to consider:

- If you have a flat-top stove or a grate that doesn't accommodate a round-bottom wok, then you need to get a flat-bottom wok. This gives you more surface area for contact with heat.
- Traditional carbon-steel woks heat quickly. You know it's preheated when there are wisps of smoke that rise from the surface. After you've swirled in the oil and let it heat for longer than a few seconds, the wisps of smoke will start ballooning. Then the wok is too hot and you will need to remove it from the heat to let it cool for a couple of minutes. If you are frying, however, you can add cool oil to even out the temperature.
- If you have a standard electric stove, you will need to add 2 to 3 minutes more to the total cooking time recommended in the recipes.
- Induction stoves vary in wattage and can be finicky, so adjust accordingly.

- A portable butane burner works well—I've used one to stir-fry outside when we visit my mother-in-law or friends who don't have big kitchens and proper exhaust systems.
- When steaming, use high heat to bring water to a boil. But then you can lower the heat to medium-high or medium for the duration of the steaming time. You want active bubbling of the water. If the steaming time is longer, it'll be important to make sure the water level doesn't go below the halfway point of the pot, or you risk drying out and scorching the pot. This has happened to me, and I not only damaged the pot but my bamboo steamer too.

餃子

Dumplings

Making Dumplings 68 | *Cooking Dumplings* 69

Classic Dumpling Dough 72

Gluten-Free Dumpling Dough 74

Tofu and Spinach Filling 76

Plant-Based "Beef" with Asparagus Filling 77

Dumpling Dipping Sauce 78

For years, I have regularly taught home cooks and culinary students how to make Chinese dumplings, including several thousand people in hands-on classes and an untold number of learners via videos and live television demonstrations. That's a lot of dumpling instruction. I have been making dumplings since I was a young child not yet able to reach the counter without standing on a stool. I'm not sure I could guess how many dumplings I've made across the decades—more than I could reasonably count or remember, but tens of thousands of dumplings is a safe guess.

All this to say that I have developed a few rules to live by in dumpling class—and beyond. I hope these reminders will not only help you manage your expectations when you delve into dumpling making but also when you try any other unfamiliar recipes and techniques in this book. The Dumpling Code is as follows:

1   **THERE ARE MANY PATHS TO THE SAME DESTINATION.** When I describe how to peel ginger, for example, I show students three options: Use a knife to cut off the skin and any rough spots. Use a vegetable peeler to shave off the skin. Use the edge of a teaspoon to scrape off the skin. This applies to any number of ways to prep other ingredients.

2   **EXPERTISE COMES FROM REPETITION.** No one can expect to be a dumpling master after one attempt at a recipe. When people tell me that I make it look easy, I have to remind them that it looks easy because I have made tens of thousands of dumplings. I still practice certain pleats that are hard to do consistently.

3   **REPETITION TEACHES YOU THE SECRETS.** Because I have made tens of thousands of dumplings, I have made mistakes and learned from them. I have had to produce dumplings in unfamiliar settings, with unpredictable circumstances and limited resources just as you might have to do.

4   **IF YOU START WITH A CIRCLE, YOU'RE MORE LIKELY TO GET A CIRCLE.** When rolling out a piece of dough to make a wrapper, if you start with a lopsided piece of dough, you will get a lopsided wrapper. But, if you roll the piece of dough into a smooth ball and flatten it between your palms to create a wafer, you will more likely roll out a round wrapper. Always try to set yourself up for success.

5   **YOU NEED THE RIGHT TOOL TO DO THE JOB WELL.** To roll dumpling wrappers efficiently, you need a Chinese rolling pin. The rolling pin makes all the difference. (See Rolling Pin, page 52.)

6   **SOMETIMES YOU HAVE TO START OVER**. Learning how to get the consistency of the dough correct can take a few tries. Sometimes you can course-correct. Other times, such as when someone eagerly pours too much water into the flour, it's better to start over. No one likes to waste food or time and energy, but there's no salvaging a dough that has turned to paste. Also see rule No. 4.

7   **NO TWO DUMPLINGS ARE EXACTLY ALIKE**. Even the most adept cooks don't produce dumplings that are carbon copies. They can be consistently shaped and have the same number of pleats, but humans aren't machines. Each dumpling is unique and they all taste good.

8   **EVEN THE BURNT ONES TASTE GOOD**. Stuff happens and life goes on. Occasionally, even now, I will get distracted and a pan of pot stickers goes beyond "caramelized" to charcoal. This happened once during a Lunar New Year party. I burned an entire pan of dumplings. I wanted to cry, because my nieces and nephews can eat a lot of dumplings and I was afraid I wouldn't have enough. But I scraped the dumplings out, hid them in a corner of the kitchen, and started over with a fresh batch. Before the end of the evening, I discovered that one of my brothers had found the plate and ate all the charred dumplings.

9   **SELF-CONSCIOUSNESS IS LEARNED**. I love teaching kids. I've observed that the younger the students, the less self-conscious they are. They are fearless when it comes to making dumplings. They know that the act of making dumplings is the goal. Adults tend to be self-critical right out of the gate. I always ask whether anyone has made dumplings and dumpling dough from scratch. In most classes, no one raises their hand. And yet, they apologize for not being perfect at a skill they've never attempted before.

10 **MAKE IT SAFE TO FAIL**. People need permission to fail. At the beginning of class, I thank everyone for coming and I remind them that we are all learning, that skill comes from repetition, and no two dumplings look the same. Our signature pleats are as individual as our fingerprints, so their dumplings won't match mine and that's okay. If they mess up the dough or burn their dumplings, it's okay. Learning means you have gained insights from something that didn't turn out as expected.

11 **NOW, GO MAKE SOME DUMPLINGS.**

Making Dumplings

Classic Dumpling Dough (page 72) is versatile and is used regardless of the filling or the cooking method. Make the dough, make one or more of the fillings (see pages 76 to 77), and proceed to fill and fold the dumplings, per the following instructions. You then can decide which cooking method you want to follow (see Cooking Dumplings, page 69). You could boil and panfry, for example, or panfry all the dumplings. It's up to you. Finally, you can serve them with dipping sauce (see page 78).

Filling Dumplings

Fill each wrapper with about 1 heaping teaspoon of your filling of choice. With a vegetable filling that doesn't have a binder, it might be challenging to rein in all the ingredients, especially the bean thread noodles. Just do your best. Homemade dumpling wrappers stretch, so you can stretch the wrapper slightly to enclose any unruly bits of vegetables.

Folding Dumplings

The simplest way to seal a dumpling is to fold the wrapper over the filling into a half-moon shape. Match the edges together and press as if you were sealing an envelope. There is no need to dab homemade wrappers with water. There is enough moisture in the dough that the edges will seal when pressed. Holding the sealed edge of the dumpling between your fingers, set it on its spine and gently wiggle it as you are pushing down so that the dumpling will stand up. Place the completed dumpling on a baking sheet lined with parchment paper. Repeat with the remaining dumplings.

To learn how to pleat the dumplings, see the step-by-step photos (page 97).

Storing Dumplings

Store leftover boiled dumplings in an airtight container. Don't pack too tightly or they will stick together once chilled. To reheat, you can dip them in boiling water to refresh or you can microwave them for 30 to 60 seconds. You also can sear them in an oiled pan over medium heat. Cover with a lid to help steam the tops of the dumplings. Alternatively, you can make Rice Cake Soup with Vegetables (page 118) and add leftover dumplings instead of the rice cake.

Cooking Dumplings

Dumplings are so versatile that you can mix and match fillings with cooking methods according to the ingredients you have available and your mood. Seeking extra comfort? Boiled dumplings, especially when piled in a bowl, send wisps of soothing steam toward your face as you take the first bites. In this way, boiled dumplings—which are also the least fussy to make—remind me of the curative properties of hot soup.

On another day, you may want the satisfaction of the crispy-chewy texture you get from pot stickers. When properly made, using a method that combines oil and water in a covered skillet, the bottom of the dumpling yields the telltale crust from frying and the top of the dumpling becomes slightly chewy from steaming. It can get a smidge greasy, but I think it's good-greasy. So many people enjoy spongy bread dipped in olive oil. A pot sticker is not so different.

For the moments when you need a more delicate experience, you might go for a steamed dumpling. Steamed dumplings are less likely to become waterlogged and they're not at all greasy—unless you include a greasy ingredient. If you don't have time to make your own wrappers and decide to use store-bought ones, steaming is your friend. It's a gentler way to cook dumplings, so if the store-bought wrappers are thin, steaming is less likely to bust the skins.

Whatever you crave, there's a dumpling for you.

Boiling Dumplings

In a large soup pot or stockpot over high heat, bring 4 quarts water to a boil. Set a 1-cup measuring cup filled with cold water next to the stove, within easy reach. When the water starts to boil, carefully add about half of the prepared dumplings, or only as many as your pot can accommodate without overcrowding. Return to a boil and then cook the dumplings for $4\frac{1}{2}$ to 5 minutes. If you are cooking frozen dumplings, boil them for 1 to 2 minutes more. Keep an eye on the water as it may bubble over, and adjust the heat as necessary. If the water starts to bubble to the top, add a splash of the cold water to tame the boil. You may need to do this a couple of times before the dumplings are finished cooking. The dumplings are done when they puff up, float, and the skins are slightly translucent. Turn down the heat to low. Using a large slotted spoon, transfer the dumplings to a platter.

Steaming Dumplings

Set up the steamer (see page 52) and bring the water to boil over high heat. Line a steamer basket with steamer paper or perforated parchment paper, and place the prepared dumplings in a single layer in the basket, leaving about 1 inch between dumplings. Place the steamer basket on top of the pot, and steam, covered, for 8 to 10 minutes, or until the wrappers puff up. If you are cooking frozen dumplings, steam them for one to two minutes more. Leftover steamed dumplings can be treated the same way as listed in the tips for boiled dumplings.

Panfrying Dumplings (Pot Stickers)

Preheat an 8- or 9-inch nonstick skillet over medium heat for about 1 minute. (If you have a bigger or smaller skillet, that's fine. Adjust the oil amount as needed.) Avoid high heat, which can cause the nonstick coating to deteriorate. A cast-iron skillet with a matching lid works well too.

Add enough vegetable oil to generously coat the entire surface of the pan and create a slight pool of oil (about 1/8 inch deep). This may seem like a lot of oil, but it will help you create that telltale crispy pot sticker crust.

Carefully arrange the dumplings in a single layer in the skillet, flat side down. Add 1/2 cup water to the skillet and cover immediately. Cook for 7 to 9 minutes, or until the water has evaporated and the bottoms of the dumplings have reached a golden brown. The cooking time may vary slightly depending on your stove. Frozen dumplings may need 1 minute more to cook. Adjust the heat as needed.

If you have leftover dumplings, store them in the refrigerator and eat within a couple of days. To reheat, place them in a lightly oiled pan over medium-low heat and let the filling come to temperature. This will refresh the crispiness of the crust. Or you can eat them cold, as I sometimes do.

PANFRY VARIATION

TO MAKE POT STICKER LACE: The best part of the pot sticker is the crispy crust. Adding starch water to the pan will create a crispy, lacy sheet of crust surrounding the pot stickers. In a small bowl, place 1 tablespoon plus 1½ teaspoons cornstarch to ½ cup water and mix to combine. Add this mixture to the pan. When the dumplings are done cooking, carefully tip the pan and use a large flexible pancake turner to help slip the dumplings and lacy crust out onto a plate. Then, invert a second plate to cover the dumplings. Carefully pick up the dumpling-plate sandwich and flip it so the lacy crust now is facing up. When you create pot sticker lace, you have to present it lace side up so everyone can appreciate its beauty—and your extra effort!

和麵
Classic Dumpling Dough

**MAKES ABOUT 1 POUND DOUGH
(FOR 45 TO 50 DUMPLINGS)**

2½ cups unbleached all-purpose flour,
plus more for dusting

¾ cup lukewarm tap water

This dough for the classic dumpling, or *jiaozi* in Mandarin, is the one I've used for decades. You can make this dough up to half a day in advance. Keep it in a covered bowl. You will have to dust it with flour and knead it to refresh it if you let it sit for more than a couple of hours. You can make the dumplings, place them on a parchment-lined tray, freeze them for thirty minutes, and then transfer to a ziplock bag to store in the freezer. Frozen dumplings should hold for one to two weeks before they start to get freezer burn or crack. When you cook them, don't defrost or you will get a soggy mess.

▪ Put the flour in a large bowl. Add the water. Using a rubber spatula, a wooden spoon, a pair of chopsticks, or your fingers, stir the water and flour together until a shaggy ball of dough starts to form. Now, use your hands to start kneading the dough and incorporating any remaining flour. The dough should feel slightly tacky but not damp. It should not stick to your fingers.

▪ Dust your work surface with flour. Remove the dough from the bowl and knead for about 2 minutes. It should feel smooth. Cover the dough with a damp towel or plastic wrap and let it rest on the counter for a minimum of 20 minutes. (While it doesn't need much longer than that, it won't hurt the dough if it happens to rest longer.)

▪ Alternatively, you can use a stand mixer to form the dough. Add the flour to the bowl of the stand mixer, and add the water gradually while running the dough hook at medium-low speed. Once the dough comes together, knead for about 2 minutes. Cover the dough and let it rest for 20 minutes. (This dough will hold for several hours at room temperature. It will get stickier, so you will have to knead in 1 to 2 tablespoons of flour to refresh it. It's best to make this dough the same day you want to use it.)

▪ Once rested, divide the dough in half. On a surface lightly dusted with flour, roll each half into a rope that's about ¾ inch in diameter and about 18 inches in length. Using a knife or a bench scraper, cut each rope into pieces that are about ¾ inch thick. Each piece should weigh 9 to 10 grams.

▪ Roll each piece of dough into a small ball and then flatten it between your palms to create a disc that resembles a wafer cookie. Press your thumb gently into the dough to create a small indentation. Position your rolling pin between you and the base of the wafer of dough. Dust lightly with flour as needed. Roll the pin forward across the dough and back. You do not need to lift the rolling pin. Turn the dough 90 degrees and repeat the forward-and-back rolling. Turn the dough 90 degrees again and repeat the rolling. This forms the beginnings of a circle.

■ Repeat this for the second revolution, but, for subsequent turns, roll the pin only halfway up. For the third revolution, roll the pin only a third of the way up. The idea is to leave the center of the circle just slightly thicker than the outer edges. The wrapper should end up being a circle about 3¼ inches in diameter. Don't worry if the circle isn't perfect; it only needs to be roundish. If it looks like an oval, then round it out. If it's lopsided beyond repair, then bunch up the dough into a ball and start again. Unless you have an assembly line of friends or family helping you, roll out about six wrappers at a time. If you roll out too many, they start to stick to each other and the edges will dry out, which makes it harder to seal.

NOTE: These dimensions are meant as a guideline. You could make these larger, if you'd like. You would end up with fewer dumplings and each would require more filling. The key is to keep the size consistent so the dumplings cook consistently. I wouldn't make these smaller, however, because it makes it more challenging to fold the dumplings, especially if you have big hands or you are a beginner.

STORE-BOUGHT DUMPLING WRAPPERS

If you don't have time to make your own wrappers, you can use store-bought round dumpling wrappers. They're also known by the Japanese term gyoza wrappers. Sometimes, you'll see the round wrappers labeled as siu mai wrappers. There are many brands available, and regular supermarkets often carry the round dumpling/gyoza wrappers and the square wonton wrappers. For *jiaozi*, the round wrappers are what you should choose. The distinction in thickness is related to the type of dumpling you're making and whether there's egg in the dough. Thin, medium, and thick dumpling wrappers are used for different cooking methods. The thinner the wrapper, the less rigorous the cooking method.

For example, you should use thin wrappers for steamed dumplings. The thicker ones are better for pot stickers because they won't tear as easily. That said, unless you are allergic to eggs, which thickness of wrapper you buy is ultimately personal preference. Any of these will get you to the end result.

The simplest way to seal the wrapper is to dab water around its circumference. Place the filling in the middle and then fold in half to align the edges and press down. This creates a half-moon shape. If you are adept at pleating, you can pleat the edges. You may need an additional dab of water to help with pleating. The cooking process is the same as described in each of the three methods on pages 69 to 70.

Gluten-Free Dumpling Dough

**MAKES ABOUT 1 POUND DOUGH
(FOR 45 TO 50 DUMPLINGS)**

2½ cups Cup4Cup Multipurpose Flour

1 cup plus 1 tablespoon warm tap water

The flavor and texture of this dough is pleasant and reminiscent of stir-fried rice cake. I find that the Cup4Cup flour requires extra water to hydrate. The flour is too gritty to use for dusting, so you will have to roll the wrappers on top of a sheet of parchment to keep it from sticking. The dough does tear if you roll it too thin, but gently press the dough back together and it will be fine.

■   In a medium bowl, combine the flour and water. Stir with a spoon or rubber spatula until the flour starts to clump. Then, using your hands, work the dough until it comes together into a ball. Knead the dough for 2 to 3 minutes, or until smooth. Return the dough to the bowl and cover the bowl with plastic wrap. Set aside.

■   Place a sheet of parchment large enough to cover your workspace. Something in the 12-by-12-inch range should do. (Since parchment comes in a variety of dimensions, use your judgment.) If needed, tape the edges of the parchment to your work surface to keep it from sliding around.

■   Divide the dough in half. Cover one half with the plastic wrap to prevent it from drying out. With the other half, roll into a rope that is about ¾ inch in diameter and roughly 18 inches in length. Using a knife or bench scraper and a cutting board, cut the rope into pieces that are about ¾ inch thick. It's equivalent to a heaping teaspoon of dough. This dough may be a little sticky. Roll each piece of dough into a small ball and then flatten it between your palms to create a disc that resembles a wafer cookie. Place on the parchment paper in front of you. Position your rolling pin between you and the base of the wafer of dough. Roll the pin forward across the dough and back. You do not need to lift the rolling pin. Turn the dough 90 degrees and repeat the forward-and-back rolling. Turn the dough 90 degrees again and repeat the rolling. This forms the beginnings of a circle.

■ Repeat this for the second revolution, but, for subsequent turns, roll the pin only halfway up. For the third revolution, roll the pin only a third of the way up. The idea is to leave the center of the circle just slightly thicker than the outer edges. The wrapper should end up being a circle about 3¼ inches in diameter. Don't worry if the circle isn't perfect; it only needs to be roundish. If the wrapper tears, just press the edges of the hole back together. Roll out up to six at a time and fill. If you roll out too many, the dough will dry out, which makes it harder to seal.

NOTE: I have not tested the full complement of off-the-shelf gluten-free flours. In addition to Cup4Cup, I have tried King Arthur Gluten-Free All-Purpose Flour, which yielded a finicky dough that didn't hold together. The flavor of the rice flour was overpowering.

Tofu and Spinach Filling

MAKES ABOUT 2⅓ CUPS FILLING

1 (12- to 14-ounce) block firm tofu, drained and cut into ½-inch-thick pieces

2 stalks green onions, chopped

1 teaspoon finely grated fresh ginger

10 ounces fresh baby spinach (about 8 cups packed), blanched for 2 minutes in simmering water, drained, and roughly chopped

¼ cup grated carrot

6 medium dried shiitake mushrooms, soaked in warm water for 2 to 3 hours, stemmed, and finely diced

2 tablespoons soy sauce

1 teaspoon garlic bean sauce

1 teaspoon sesame oil

⅛ teaspoon white pepper powder

The particulars of this filling are flexible. You can add different spices, exchange greens, or trade for another type of mushroom or combine mushrooms. Let your produce bin or your cravings decide.

■ Place the tofu in the bowl of a food processor. Pulse several times to break up the tofu. Add the onions, ginger, baby spinach, carrot, mushrooms, soy sauce, garlic bean sauce, oil, and white pepper powder. Pulse for a few seconds at a time until the ingredients become integrated but still coarse. Be careful not to overprocess because you don't want a paste. The ingredients should still be discernible.

■ As the filling rests, some of the liquid from the tofu and/or the spinach may pool at the bottom of the bowl. That's okay. You can drain it or take a clean paper towel and dab it to absorb the excess liquid.

素牛肉餡

Plant-Based "Beef"

with Asparagus Filling

MAKES ABOUT 1 POUND FILLING

1 pound plant-based ground beef

1 cup finely chopped asparagus

1 stalk green onion, finely chopped

2 tablespoons soy sauce

1 tablespoon sesame oil

1½ teaspoons garlic bean sauce

1 teaspoon minced fresh ginger

⅛ teaspoon white pepper powder

Vegetable fillings can be delicious, but the ingredients don't naturally bind together like meats do. That can sometimes make it messy when trying to contain a filling within the confines of a dumpling wrapper. If you enjoy plant-based ground beef, or you're willing to give it a try, this filling mimics the texture of a regular meat filling. The pungent seasonings give the flavor a kick.

■   In a medium bowl, combine the ground beef, asparagus, onion, soy sauce, oil, garlic bean sauce, ginger, and white pepper powder. Mix well.

ALTERNATIVES: To make this gluten-free, use a gluten-free soy sauce or tamari. If you can't find a gluten-free garlic bean sauce, you can use 1 teaspoon crushed fresh garlic. To make this filling soy-free, be sure to use a soy-free plant-based ground beef. Instead of soy sauce and garlic bean sauce, use 1 teaspoon kosher salt and 1 teaspoon crushed fresh garlic.

Dumpling Dipping Sauce

MAKES ABOUT ⅓ CUP

⅓ cup soy sauce

2 tablespoons unseasoned rice vinegar

1 stalk green onion, finely chopped

2 large cloves garlic, finely chopped or crushed

1 tablespoon chopped fresh cilantro

1 teaspoon minced fresh ginger

1 teaspoon chili sauce (optional)

This is my classic dumpling dipping sauce that's always a hit. You can make it gluten-free by using a gluten-free tamari or soy sauce. Do read the label carefully because not all tamari sauces are 100 percent gluten-free. If you have a soy allergy, you can use coconut aminos to make the sauce. While coconut aminos is too sweet for stir-fries, it works well for the dipping sauce, where a hint of sweetness is balanced by the other ingredients. Using different vinegars is a way to change the flavor profile too.

■ In a small bowl, combine the soy sauce, vinegar, onion, garlic, cilantro, ginger, and chili sauce. Set aside on the counter for at least 30 minutes, if possible, to let the flavors meld together. The longer the mixture rests, the more intense the flavor becomes. You can store the dipping sauce in a sealed container in the refrigerator for up to 1 week.

中式小點

Dim Sum and Small Bites

Crystal Dumplings with Squash and Peas 85

Flaky Ribbon Pancakes 89

Spring Rolls 92

Soup Dumplings 95

Sticky Rice in Lotus Leaf 99

Steamed Vegetable Baozi 103

Red Bean Soup 105

Everyday Chinese meals don't follow the construct of appetizer, main course, dessert. Everything is family-style, so the food arrives when it arrives. By the time the last item shows up, the table is likely so packed you have to stack a plate or two. What this means is that your dumplings might be next to a main dish, which might be next to a tureen of soup. And that's part of the energy of a group meal. Everyone sits around a table with a lazy Susan and spins to the dishes they want to eat. But instead of serving themselves, it's customary to serve their neighbors first. Even in an informal setting, there are still some rituals of etiquette.

Usually, it's only during a formal banquet, such as a wedding, where the meal is served by course. In that case, the first course is often a cold plate that's arranged with an assortment of cooked and chilled meats, seasoned nuts, quick pickles, Chinese-style salads, and such. There are specially designed, sometimes ornate platters that are reserved for this purpose. What the West might categorize as appetizers are snacks that you would have with tea. That's what dim sum is, after all. Those steamed buns and little dishes of savory dumplings, ribs, tofu rolls, rice noodle rolls, and everything we all love are a collection of snacks, many of which are popular street foods that you can enjoy at any time of the day.

The recipes that follow are ones that can be adapted for different combinations of fillings or seasonings. Spring rolls have incredible flexibility when it comes to fillings. You can dress them up or down. Instead of shiitake mushrooms, maybe you splurge on morels. Baozi have a similar flexibility. You can switch fillings between, say, steamed vegetable baozi and vegetable dumplings, or the wontons and the crystal dumplings. The method is the same regardless of what's inside the baozi or dumpling. The ribbon pancake has room for interpretation too. There are different methods for making the dough and for how to fold and twist the dough to create flaky layers. Some use a roux, some use just oil, and some include sesame seeds. Like any bread or flatbread, there are variations.

As for when to serve dim sum and little bites, it's up to you. You are certainly welcome to present any of these snacks as an appetizer course. Or you can serve a selection of them for brunch, lunch, cocktail hour, or late-night snacks.

水晶餃

Crystal Dumplings

with Squash and Peas

MAKES ABOUT 18 DUMPLINGS

For the filling:

¾ cup frozen butternut squash

1 cup water

¼ cup frozen peas and carrots, soaked in hot water for 5 to 10 minutes

¼ cup finely chopped fresh mushrooms, such as oyster or beech

½ teaspoon kosher salt

1 teaspoon grated fresh ginger

1 teaspoon crushed fresh garlic

1 stalk green onion, finely chopped

¼ teaspoon sesame oil

⅛ teaspoon white pepper powder

For the dough:

1 cup wheat starch

⅓ cup tapioca starch

⅔ cup water

1 tablespoon vegetable shortening

For rolling:

Parchment paper and a cleaver (or a tortilla press or large flat-bottomed glass)

For serving:

Soy sauce

If you eat shrimp, you've likely had *har gow*, the shrimp dumpling that's a popular item on the dim sum cart. This vegetarian version uses the same dough for the wrappers and the filling is a mix of butternut squash and peas and carrots. Fair warning: These are fussy dumplings. The dough is particular and delicate, which means it takes patience and self-forgiveness to make these. Allow yourself plenty of time to make these and absolutely do not try them for the first time when you plan on having guests over. If you have access to food-safe rubber gloves, a pair will come in handy when mixing the dough.

■ To make the filling, combine the butternut squash and water in a small pot. Bring to a boil over high heat, then reduce the heat to low. Let the squash steam, stirring occasionally, for 3 to 5 minutes, or until cooked through. Drain any liquid, then gently mash the squash with a fork or a potato masher until there are no more large chunks. The intent is not to have a puree but a mash. Transfer to a medium bowl. Drain the peas and carrots, and add to the squash. Add the mushrooms, salt, ginger, garlic, onion, oil, and white pepper powder. Stir well to combine. Set aside.

■ To make the dough, stir together the wheat starch and tapioca starch in a large heatproof bowl. In a small pot, bring the water to a roiling boil. The water must reach at least 212 degrees F. With a rubber spatula or wooden spoon in one hand, use the other hand to carefully add the boiling-hot water to the starches. Immediately start stirring to form the dough. Continue to stir until a ball of dough starts to form. If you have food-safe rubber gloves, this would be a good time to use them to help you knead the dough. If you don't have gloves, you can continue to use the rubber spatula or carefully use bare hands. Add the vegetable shortening and knead the dough to incorporate. Since it's a starch dough and we're not concerned about developing elasticity, it's not necessary to knead for very long.

■ Roll out the dough into a rope that is roughly 18 inches long and about 1 inch in diameter. Cut into 16 to 18 even pieces. Each piece of dough will be 12 to 14 grams. Roll each piece of dough into a smooth ball. Cover loosely with a piece of plastic wrap to prevent the dough from drying out.

→

■ Cut two pieces of parchment paper that are 6 inches square. Place one piece of dough in the middle of one sheet of parchment. Cover with the other piece of parchment. Use the flat side of a cleaver (or use a tortilla press or flat-bottomed glass) and press down firmly to form a disc that's about ⅛ inch thick. Peel the wrapper away from the parchment carefully. Place about 1 teaspoon of the squash filling in the center. Carefully fold the skin in half and join the edges of the wrapper, pinching flat to seal. You will get a half-moon shape. Because there's zero elasticity in the dough, it can tear very easily. If you are experienced at pleating dumplings, you can work in some pleats. Repeat with the remaining pieces of dough and filling.

■ Place the completed dumplings on a parchment-lined baking tray. Cover the tray loosely with another piece of plastic wrap as you are making the dumplings to keep the dumplings from drying out. It is best to make and steam these dumplings the same day. You can freeze the dumplings and steam them frozen. The caveat is that the dough is finicky and the process of freezing may crack the surface.

■ To steam, set up the steamer and bring the water to a boil over high heat. Line the steamer with steamer paper (see page 54) and arrange the dumplings in a single layer in the steamer basket. Leave about 1 inch of space between dumplings. They won't expand, but you don't want them to stick together. When the water is boiling, reduce the heat to medium and place the steamer basket on the pot and cover. Steam for 5 to 7 minutes, or until the skins are translucent. Serve while hot with soy sauce on the side.

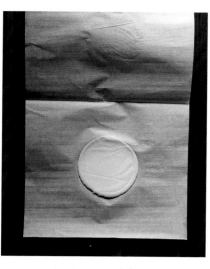

Flaky Ribbon Pancakes

MAKES 4 PANCAKES

For the dough:

2½ cups all-purpose flour, plus more for flouring

1 teaspoon kosher salt

¾ cup warm tap water, roughly 90 degrees F

For the roux:

¼ cup vegetable oil

¼ cup all-purpose flour

For the pancakes:

2 teaspoons kosher salt

3 stalks green onions, finely chopped, divided into 4 portions

1 teaspoon toasted sesame seeds (optional), divided

4 teaspoons vegetable oil

Dumpling Dipping Sauce (page 78)

The Chinese name for these pancakes is *shou* (hand or fingers) *zhua* (grab or catch) *bing* (pancake). It's similar to the Indian paratha and the term has been adopted by some Chinese. In fact, you might see packages of frozen pancakes labeled as parathas at an Asian market. Conceptually, it's a pancake that has layers of ribbons coiled within it and you use your fingers to pull a stretch of pancake and break it off to eat. There are many variations on the method for producing these pancakes. Some involve intricate fan folds or require multiple resting periods for the dough or dipping in egg and so on. The bottom line is that it's a flaky flatbread. No matter how you get there, it's delicious.

■　To make the dough, combine the flour and salt in a medium bowl. Swirl in the water and stir with a rubber spatula to combine. Then, using your hands, gather and knead the dough together to create a ball. It will look shaggy. If it isn't coming together, you may need a splash more water. Add about 1 tablespoon water and see if that helps. If not, add 1 more tablespoon. If the dough is too damp and sticks to your hands goopily, then work in 1 tablespoon flour. The texture should be tacky but not wet. Dust your work surface with flour. Knead the dough for 1 to 2 minutes. It will still look a bit rough, but it will smooth out once the dough has had a chance to rest. Place the dough in the bowl and drape a damp tea towel over the bowl or use a piece of plastic wrap to cover. Let rest for 30 minutes.

■　In the meantime, make the roux by heating the oil in a small pan over medium heat. When the surface of the oil starts to shimmer, turn off the heat. In a small heatproof bowl, add the flour. Pour the hot oil over the flour and stir immediately, but carefully, to combine. Continue stirring until well combined. Set aside to cool while the dough finishes resting.

■　Once the dough has rested, knead it for 1 minute, or until it's smooth. Place the dough on the counter or your workbench. Divide the dough into 4 equal pieces, about 4½ ounces each. Working with one piece at a time, roll out the dough until it is a rectangle roughly 10 inches by 5 inches, with the long edge facing you. To begin making the pancakes, brush a thin coating of the roux on the dough. Sprinkle on ¼ teaspoon of the salt and 1 portion of the onions. Add ¼ teaspoon of the sesame seeds.

- To fold the pancakes, imagine what a trifold brochure looks like. You will mimic that shape with the dough. Starting on the bottom edge, fold up one-third of the way. Then fold the top edge down to overlap. Now you have a strip of dough. Visualize about a 1-inch border on each of the short edges. With a sharp knife, make two evenly spaced cuts down the length of this strip of dough, without cutting through those 1-inch borders. The goal is to have "tabs" on the end that you can hold, but there will be three strands of dough in the middle.

- Picking up the ends of the dough, gently stretch until the strands are about 20 inches long. Starting from one end, roll the dough into a tight coil, making sure to keep the strands of dough from splaying out. When you get to the end, turn the dough so that it stands up on one of the coiled sides. Tuck the loose end under the bottom side of the coil and press to secure. Now, using the palm of your hand, press down firmly on the coil to flatten. Use a rolling pin to roll out the coil until it is about 6 inches in diameter and about ¼ inch thick. Set aside and repeat the process with the remaining dough.

- Preheat an 8-inch nonstick or cast-iron skillet over medium heat for about 1 minute. Reduce the heat to low. Drizzle 1 teaspoon of the vegetable oil on the skillet and swirl to coat. Place a pancake in the skillet, cover with a lid, and let cook for 2 to 3 minutes, or until golden brown. Flip the pancake and cook the other side for another 2 minutes, or until golden brown. Pay attention to the heat and adjust as needed. You don't want the pancakes to brown too quickly. Repeat with the remaining pancakes.

- As the pancakes come out of the pan, you want to scrunch the sides together to loosen the inner ribbons. There are a few ways to do that. You can use your hands if you wear some oven mitts. Or you can use two sturdy spatulas or a pair of large tongs. Serve the scrunched pancakes on a platter, with dipping sauce on the side. It's finger food!

Spring Rolls

MAKES ABOUT 1 DOZEN

1 small bundle bean thread noodles, soaked in warm water for 10 minutes to reconstitute

2 tablespoons vegetable oil, plus more for frying

2½ cups thinly sliced Chinese cabbage

1 medium carrot, cut into thin, 2-inch-long strips (about ¾ cup)

6 medium fresh or dried shiitake mushrooms (if using dried, soak in warm water to reconstitute), thinly sliced

2 stalks green onions, finely chopped

¼ cup water

3 tablespoons soy sauce

Kosher salt

½ teaspoon sesame oil

½ cup chopped fresh cilantro (optional)

1 package 8-inch spring roll wrappers, such as Wei-Chuan or TYJ brands

1 egg, beaten

Sweet-and-Sour Sauce (recipe follows), for serving

Soy sauce, for serving

Chili sauce or sweet chili sauce, for serving

Crispy spring rolls are so ubiquitous on menus across many types of Asian restaurants that it hardly seems worth it to make your own. But here's why it is worth it: because it tastes better. In restaurants, the spring rolls tend to be small and contain filler ingredients that may not contribute much flavor. They're treated like the vehicles for sweet chili sauce that they are. If you're unlucky, the spring rolls arrive drenched with hot oil—which tells you the fryer oil was not at the right temperature. That's not to say that a home cook is immune from similar issues. But at least you can control what goes inside the spring rolls.

■ Drain the bean thread. Cut the bean thread bundle into 3 to 4 segments so the noodles aren't whole but also aren't too short.

■ In a wok or large skillet, heat the vegetable oil over medium-high heat. Add the cabbage, carrots, mushrooms, and onions, and stir-fry the vegetables for 1 minute, or until the cabbage has cooked through. Add the bean thread, water, and soy sauce, stir to combine, and cook for 2 to 3 minutes, or until the bean thread have absorbed the sauce. Add salt to taste. Drizzle with the oil and add the cilantro. Give everything a good toss to combine. Transfer the filling to a large bowl and set aside to cool for a few minutes.

■ Position a sheet of spring roll wrapper with a corner toward you so that it's like a diamond. Place about ¼ cup filling about 2 inches above the bottom corner of the wrapper. Fold the bottom corner up over the filling and roll about halfway up. Fold the right-side "flap" over the filling, then the left side. Brush the top flap with egg and then finish rolling to seal. Repeat with the remaining wrappers and filling.

■ In a deep pan, add about 1½ inches of vegetable oil, and heat over high heat to 375 degrees F on an instant-read thermometer. In two batches, fry the rolls for 2 minutes per side, or until the skin is evenly brown. If the skin browns too quickly, then the oil is too hot. Adjust the stove as needed.

■ Serve immediately with a selection of condiments, including Sweet-and-Sour Sauce, soy sauce, and your favorite bottled chili sauce or sweet chili sauce.

Sweet-and-Sour Sauce

MAKES ABOUT 1 CUP

⅓ cup ketchup

⅓ cup sugar, plus more as needed

⅓ cup white vinegar

This sweet-and-sour sauce is based on the version that we served in my family's restaurant. The restaurant version contained red dye, however, which earned it the nickname "red sauce." I leave out the dye—it's not necessary—and I don't add thickener. But, if you prefer a thicker sauce, I include instructions for how to thicken it.

■ In a small pot over medium heat, combine the ketchup, sugar, and vinegar, and stir until the sugar dissolves and the sauce becomes syrupy and slightly thickened, 5 to 7 minutes. Add a little more sugar, if desired, then let cool and serve. Store leftover sauce in a covered jar in the refrigerator for up to 1 week.

■ If the sauce is too runny for your preference, you can thicken it with a cornstarch slurry. Mix 2 tablespoons cornstarch with 3 tablespoons water. Stir into the sauce toward the end, making sure to combine well. Let simmer for 1 minute, or until thickened. Remove from heat and let cool to room temperature.

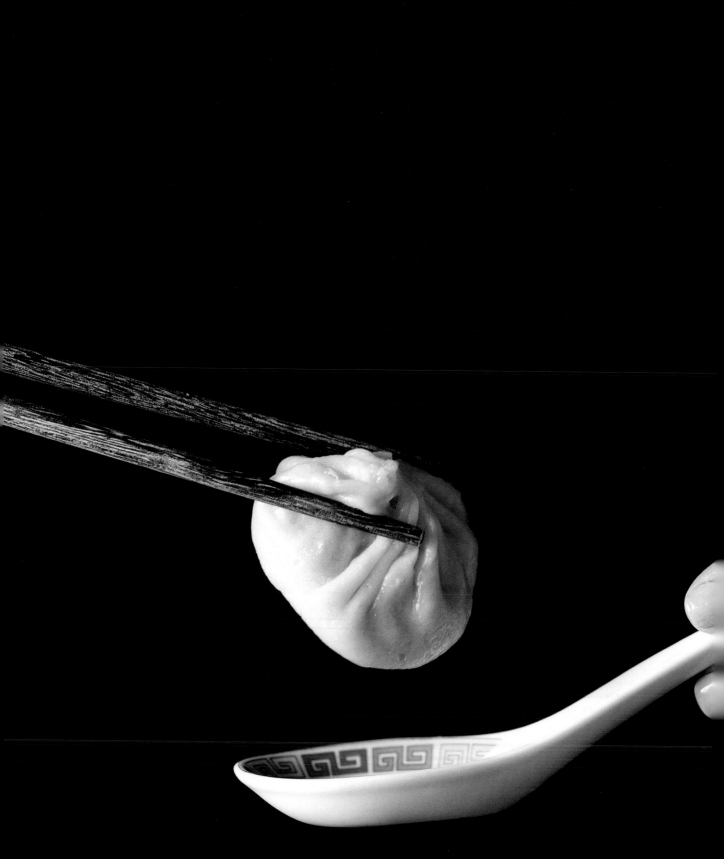

素 小 籠 包

Soup Dumplings

MAKES ABOUT 40 SOUP DUMPLINGS

For the gelatin:

6 dried shiitake mushrooms

1 stalk green onion, trimmed and cut into 3-inch-long segments

2 thin slices ginger, roughly the size of a quarter

1 tablespoon Shaoxing wine, optional

1 tablespoon soy sauce

6 cups water

Salt

2 envelopes Knox gelatin

For the filling:

1 tablespoon vegetable oil

2 stalks green onions, finely chopped

2 cloves garlic, finely chopped

10 ounces fresh baby spinach (about 8 cups packed), roughly chopped

1 tablespoon water

1 cup grated carrots (about 2 medium carrots)

6 medium dried shiitake mushrooms, soaked in warm water for 2 to 3 hours to reconstitute, finely diced (about ½ cup)

Ingredients continued on next page

Soup dumplings (aka *xiao long bao* or XLB) have been enjoying a fervent following in the United States in the last few years. There have been many debates about which restaurants have the best-quality soup dumplings. Traditionally, the filling consists of pork and the juicy broth that starts as a gelatin when mixed into the filling and melts when steamed. Here, we have a tofu-based filling and a simple vegetable broth that gels with the addition of agar agar, a seaweed-based product. Making soup dumplings requires advance work to make the gelatin, so plan accordingly. The dough and wrappers must be handmade. Using store-bought gyoza/dumpling wrappers won't work if your intention is to achieve the signature top knot on the dumpling. When serving, you can dip the soup dumplings in the traditional Chinese black vinegar, or you can make the Dumpling Dipping Sauce (page 78) to serve with it instead.

■ To make the gelatin, combine the mushrooms, onion, ginger, wine, soy sauce, and water in a 3-quart pot. Bring to a boil and then lower the heat. Let the liquid simmer for about 20 minutes. Taste the broth and season for salt. Start with ½ teaspoon salt and add more to taste. You want the broth to have just enough savory flavor, but you don't want it to be too salty. You will need just 2 cups of the broth. You can save the rest to make another soup.

■ Combine 2 cups of the hot broth with the Knox gelatin in a small pot over low heat. Whisk constantly until the gelatin dissolves completely. Let cool until you can transfer to a baking dish or storage container. Cover with plastic wrap or a lid and refrigerate until chilled and set, at least several hours or overnight.

■ To make the filling, preheat a wok over high heat until wisps of smoke rise from the surface. Swirl in the vegetable oil and immediately add the green onions and garlic. Stir vigorously for 10 seconds. Add the spinach and water, and stir-fry for about 30 seconds to cook the spinach. Add the carrots, mushrooms, and bean thread. Stir to combine. Turn the heat to medium low, add the soy sauce, and stir to combine. Add salt to taste, if needed. Add the sesame oil. Stir once again and transfer the filling to a medium bowl. Dig a hole in the middle of the filling and spread it up the wall of the bowl. This will help it cool more quickly. Place in the refrigerator and chill until cool. If the filling is hot, it will melt the gelatin.

→

1 small bundle bean thread noodles, soaked in warm water for 10 minutes to soften and roughly chopped (about 1 cup)

2 tablespoons soy sauce

Kosher salt

½ teaspoon sesame oil

For the dough:

2 cups all-purpose flour, plus more for dusting

½ cup bread flour

¾ cup plus 1 tablespoon hot water (150 to 160 degrees F)

For dipping:

Chinese black vinegar and julienned fresh ginger, to taste

■ Finely mince enough of the gelatin to get about 1½ cups. Add the minced gelatin to the filling and stir well to combine.

■ To make the dough, put the all-purpose flour and bread flour in a large bowl, and stir to combine. Gradually add half the water while stirring with a spatula or a pair of chopsticks. As the dough comes together, add more water. You may or may not need all of the water. Press the dough together; if you can form a ball, you can stop adding water. Form a ball and knead the dough for 4 minutes, or until smooth. Cover the bowl with a damp towel and let the dough rest for 30 minutes at room temperature.

■ On a lightly floured work surface, knead the dough again for 2 minutes, or until smooth. Divide the dough into 2 portions. Cover one half with a damp towel. Roll the other half into a rope about 1 inch in diameter. Cut the rope into pieces about 1 inch long or about 10 grams each. Using a Chinese rolling pin (dowel), roll out each piece of dough into a 3½-inch round. Place about 1 tablespoon of the filling in the center of the wrapper. Gather the edges and twist into a "top knot" above the center of the dumpling (see photo on page 94). Place each dumpling in the steamer basket, leaving about 1 inch of space between dumplings. Repeat with the remaining dough and filling. If you don't have enough steamer baskets, place the sealed dumplings on a parchment-lined baking sheet.

■ Set up the steamer and bring the water to boil over high heat. Line the steamer with steamer paper (see page 54) and arrange the dumplings in a single layer in the steamer basket.

■ Steam the dumplings (see page 52) over high heat for 6 to 8 minutes, depending on the size of the dumplings. When done steaming, the dough will transform from opaque to slightly translucent.

■ Serve immediately, straight from the steamer basket, with vinegar or dipping sauce.

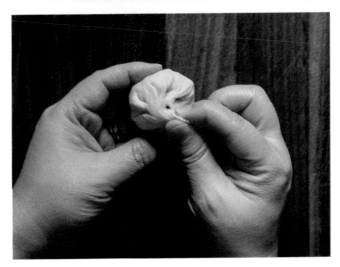

荷葉糯米飯

Sticky Rice in Lotus Leaf

MAKES 4 PACKETS

For the rice:

2 (8-ounce) cups sweet rice

Water, as needed

For the lotus leaves:

2 whole lotus leaves

For the filling:

3 tablespoons vegetable oil, divided

2 cups minced baby bok choy

½ cup minced carrot

1 heaping cup chopped fresh oyster mushrooms, or a mix of mushrooms, such as oyster, shiitake, beech, and/ or enoki

2 stalks green onions, finely chopped

2½ tablespoons soy sauce

½ teaspoon sesame oil

⅛ teaspoon white pepper powder

For serving:

Chili sauce (optional)

Unwrapping a lotus leaf packet is like opening a present. It's always fresh from the steamer and takes quick fingers and a pair of chopsticks to flick open the flaps to reveal the sticky rice within. Then you have to break apart the mound of rice to extract the perfect bite of filling and rice, which absorbs herbal notes from the lotus leaf. Usually, you wrap soaked, uncooked sweet rice into the lotus leaf and steam for ninety minutes or more. This requires a long soaking time (several hours to overnight). My shortcut is to cook the rice first, which reduces the steaming time to about fifteen minutes. Using the rice cooker has allowed me to reduce the amount of soaking time to as little as thirty minutes.

■   To prepare the rice, rinse the rice in several changes of water and drain. If using a rice cooker, follow the instructions for cooking 4 rice-cooker cups of sweet rice.

■   If using the stove-top method, place the rice in a medium Dutch oven and add water to about ½ inch above the rice. Cover the pot with a lid and bring to a boil over high heat. Don't walk away during this time. Reduce the heat to low. Cock the lid slightly to let the steam escape as you cook. Let cook for 30 to 45 minutes, or until the water has been absorbed and the rice grains look plump. Remove the pot from the heat and let the rice rest in the pot, covered, for 10 to 15 minutes to let the rice finish steaming.

■   Meanwhile, soak the lotus leaves in warm tap water in a large container or a very clean sink. By the time the rice is done cooking, the lotus leaves should be pliable.

■   To make the filling, preheat a wok over high heat until wisps of smoke rise from the surface. Add 1 tablespoon of the vegetable oil and heat until it starts to shimmer. Add the baby bok choy, carrot, mushrooms, and onions, and stir-fry for about 1 minute. Add the soy sauce and stir-fry for 1 to 2 minutes more. Drizzle on the sesame oil and add the white pepper powder. Stir to combine. Remove from the heat and transfer the vegetable mixture to a medium bowl to cool slightly. Set aside.

■   To prepare the lotus leaves, you will likely need only one whole leaf. The extra is just in case a piece tears. Open up a lotus leaf. It will be large and round. Using scissors, cut the leaf in half so there are two fans. Then, cut each of the fans in half to create quarter wedges. Place the leaves light side down

→

and green side up. Using a clean tea towel or a paper towel, dab dry the green side of the leaves. With a pastry brush and the remaining 2 tablespoons oil, brush the green side of the leaves with a thin layer of oil.

■ Place about ½ cup of the cooked rice on the oiled leaf. Add ¼ cup of the filling and top with another ½ cup of the cooked rice. Fold the sides of the leaves over the rice, overlapping the flaps to create a square or rectangular packet. You can tie it with kitchen twine, if you'd like, but I usually place the packet with the flap side down and let the weight of the rice keep the packet closed. Repeat with the remaining 3 sheets of leaves.

■ Set up the steamer and bring the water to boil over high heat. Meanwhile, place the packets, folded side down, in the steamer basket. You may have to use two steamer baskets or do it in batches. Once the water comes to a boil, reduce the heat to medium. Place the steamer baskets on the steamer pot. Steam for about 15 minutes. Serve hot, with chili sauce on the side.

素蒸包

Steamed Vegetable Baozi

MAKES 8 BAOZI

For the dough:

2¼ teaspoons active dry yeast

1 teaspoon sugar

¼ cup warm water, about 110 degrees F

2 cups all-purpose flour, plus more for dusting

¾ cup cake flour

1 tablespoon baking powder

½ cup room-temperature water

1 teaspoon vegetable oil

For the filling:

4 cups water

1 bundle bean thread noodles, soaked in warm water for 10 minutes and roughly chopped

2 cups finely chopped greens, such as baby bok choy or yu choy

2 stalks green onions, finely chopped

6 medium shiitake mushrooms, soaked for 2 to 3 hours, stemmed, and finely chopped

½ cup diced, ¼-inch, spiced tofu

1½ teaspoons kosher salt

1 teaspoon sesame oil

⅛ teaspoon white pepper powder

8 (2-inch-square) pieces parchment paper

This is not something you make on the spur of the moment. But it's one of those perfect foods that can sate your hunger, warm your insides, and soothe your soul. My mother is the one who craves vegetable baozi (the rest of my family prefer meat-filled or red bean–filled baozi) and I make these for her. She's not very demanding, so when she requests baozi, I jump to it with pleasure. Store any leftovers in an airtight container in the refrigerator and either steam to reheat or microwave them for thirty to sixty seconds.

■　To make the dough, combine the yeast, sugar, and warm water in a small bowl and stir to combine. Let sit for about 5 minutes. In a medium bowl, combine both flours and the baking powder. Stir in the yeast mixture and room-temperature water, and work until a ball of dough forms. Knead the dough for 5 minutes, or until smooth. Brush the sides of a large bowl with the vegetable oil. Place the ball of dough in the oiled bowl. Cover the bowl with plastic wrap and put in a warm place, such as the oven or by a heat vent. If you have a proofing setting for your oven, set it for 80 to 90 degrees F. Let the dough rise for 1 to 1½ hours, or until it doubles in size.

■　Meanwhile, make the filling. Bring the 4 cups water to a boil in a medium pot over high heat. Reduce heat to low. Add the bean thread, greens, onions, mushrooms, and spiced tofu. Let blanch for 3 minutes. Drain well and place the ingredients in a medium bowl. Add the salt, sesame oil, and white pepper powder, and mix well. Cover loosely with plastic wrap and set aside.

■　Place the dough on your work surface and knead it for 2 minutes, or until smooth. Divide the dough into 8 pieces. Dust lightly with flour. Roll each piece into a ball and then press the dough between your palms to flatten. Using your fingers, stretch out the dough until it's roughly 3½ inches in diameter.

■　Place 1 to 2 tablespoons of filling in the center of the dough. It should be pretty full and you should have to stretch the edge of the wrapper over the filling. Now, visualize what a drawstring bag looks like and how it functions. You are trying to create a similar shape when you seal the baozi, except you aren't cinching the baozi's "neck." Instead, you are taking the very edge of the dough and pleating it like a tiny paper fan. Start on one side and pinch the edge together as you work your way around. When you get to the end, you will have gathered the edges at a central point. If you've ever had a baozi, you should have an impression of what shape you're trying to achieve. It doesn't

→

have to be perfect or resemble the uniformity of a restaurant baozi. Place the baozi on a parchment square in the steamer basket. Repeat with the remaining dough and filling. When done, put the lid on the steamer basket and let the baozi rest for about 30 minutes.

■ Meanwhile, set up your steamer and bring the water to a boil over high heat. Reduce the heat to medium. After the baozi have rested, place the steamer basket(s) on the steamer and steam for 10 minutes. Turn off the heat, but let the baozi rest in the residual heat for 5 minutes. Serve while hot.

紅豆湯

Red Bean Soup

MAKES ABOUT 2½ CUPS SOUP

10 ounces Chinese red beans or Japanese adzuki beans

3 cups water, for soaking

12 cups water, divided, for cooking

¾ cup sugar

For a kid who did not like beans, I sure ate (and still eat) a lot of red bean soup and red bean paste–filled buns and pastries. Perhaps it's because the beans are sweetened and associated with pastries. I usually buy the tiny red beans that are a touch bigger than lentils. But the larger adzuki beans work well too. If you want to get even more "hardcore," you can buy frozen glutinous rice balls to add to this snack. Cook the glutinous rice balls according to the package instructions and then add to the red bean soup. While it's called a soup, we don't treat this like a savory broth-based soup. It's a sweet treat. If you have leftover beans, you can mash them to make red bean paste. This paste can be used to make red bean steamed buns. Use the dough technique in the Steamed Vegetable Baozi recipe (page 103) and use the red bean paste instead of the vegetable filling.

■ Place the red beans in a large bowl. Add the 3 cups water and soak for at least 2 hours. Drain and place in a large Dutch oven. Add 6 cups of the water and bring the pot to a boil over high heat. Reduce the heat to low and let the beans simmer, with the lid on the pot slightly cocked, for 2 to 2½ hours, or until the beans are soft and broken. After about 1 hour of simmering, stir in the remaining 6 cups water. Throughout the cooking process, check on the beans, stirring occasionally to make sure nothing is sticking. It's done when the beans are mashable. The consistency should still be slightly soupy. If it isn't, stir in 1 cup water to loosen it up.

■ When the beans are tender and mashable, stir in the sugar. While stirring, gently mash some of the beans. If you are adding cooked glutinous rice balls as suggested in the headnote, then add them at this time. Turn off the heat. Taste the beans. If you prefer it sweeter, you can add more sugar to taste. Serve in small soup bowls.

湯品及燉燒

Soups and Braises

Vegetable Broth 109

Ginger-Red Date Broth 110

Braised Chinese Cabbage and Fried Shallots 111

Mian Pian Soup 113

Hot-and-Sour Soup with Dried Lily Flowers 114

Braised Daikon 115

Chinese Purple Seaweed and Tofu Soup 116

Rice Cake Soup with Vegetables 118

Vegetarian Wonton Soup 119

Sweet Corn Soup 123

**Taiwanese Cabbage and Tomato Soup
with Bean Thread Noodles** 124

Braised Bamboo Shoots and Shiitake Mushrooms 127

Soups can play several positions within the course of a Chinese meal. It can start a meal, accompany a meal, be the meal, or chase a meal. A hearty soup, filled with a generous amount of chunky vegetables and sliced rice cake, might be better suited as part of the meal. A thick, elemental concoction, such as corn soup, might be the remedy for someone who is under the weather. A light, aromatic broth, on the other hand, might be served as an accompaniment during or at the end of a meal to wash down richer bites of food. Because it's meant to serve as a palate cleanser, clear broths are intentionally seasoned lightly.

Of course, noodle soups are meals unto their own that might appear at breakfast, lunch, dinner, or as a late-night snack. You don't have to ask me twice if I'd be up for a bowl of noodle soup. The noodles are filling, and the piping-hot soup sends savory aromas through your olfactory system and soothes your insides going down. If anything is soulful, it's noodle soups, and they represent a universal language among the Chinese, if not across many Asian cultures. Many noodle soups are quite humble, with light broths and simple vegetables or pickles. They're not meant to impress thrill seekers, but they are unquestionably sustaining.

Versatility and function are as much hallmarks as deliciousness when it comes to Chinese soups. Long hours of simmering aren't necessary to extract the fresh aromas from ingredients. I so appreciate such efficiency because it takes just minutes to create something that's warming and satisfying. Some soups don't even need to begin with vegetable broth. Water can easily be transformed into a vehicle for flavors, with a few aromatic ingredients, such as green onions, ginger, and perhaps celery or chopped fresh tomatoes.

Vegetable braises (or Chinese casseroles) have a similar demeanor in that they need to simmer only as long as it takes for the main ingredient to become tender. The sturdy daikon takes a little longer to cook down, but the braising time is still less than an hour. Vegetable braises remind me that there is so much intrinsic flavor in vegetables and that they often are obliterated by stronger seasonings. You can really taste the sweetness of Chinese cabbage when you braise it. I marvel at this alchemy every time.

素菜湯

Vegetable Broth

MAKES 4 TO 6 CUPS BROTH

8 cups water

2 squares dried kelp, about 1 gram

½ cup bean sprouts

4 medium dried shiitake mushrooms

1 rib celery, an inner, lighter-green stalk, cut in half

The beauty of vegetable broth is that it doesn't take very long to make. Use this as a base for soup or as a substitute in any stir-fry that calls for water. You can make a double or triple batch and freeze in smaller quantities.

■ In a medium pot, combine the water, kelp, bean sprouts, mushrooms, and celery. Bring to a boil over high heat. Reduce the heat to medium low and simmer for 15 to 20 minutes. Strain before using. If serving as an accompaniment, season with salt to taste.

紅棗薑湯

Ginger-Red Date Broth

MAKES 4 TO 6 CUPS BROTH

8 cups water

1 stalk green onion, cut into 3-inch-long segments

2 to 3 coin-shaped slices ginger, about ¼ inch thick

4 Chinese dried red dates

1 rib celery, an inner, lighter-green stalk, cut in half

The dried dates offer a hint of sweetness that counters the pungency of the aromatics. It serves nicely as a base for Vegetarian Wonton Soup (page 119). But you could add some soy sauce or salt to this broth and drink it on its own.

■ In a medium pot, combine the water, onion, ginger, dates, and celery. Bring to a boil over high heat. Reduce the heat to medium low and simmer for 15 to 20 minutes. Strain before using. If serving as an accompaniment, season with salt to taste.

紅蔥酥燒大白菜

Braised Chinese Cabbage and Fried Shallots

MAKES 4 SERVINGS

1 pound Chinese cabbage, cut into 1-inch-thick slices

4 cups water

1 teaspoon soy sauce

¼ cup fried shallots, plus more garnish, if desired (store-bought is fine)

1 bundle bean thread noodles, soaked in warm water for 10 minutes (optional)

¾ teaspoon kosher salt, or to taste

⅛ teaspoon white pepper powder

Suggested pairings: Meatless Ma Po Tofu (page 206) and Spiced Tofu with Leeks and Cabbage (page 203)

One of my favorite ways to eat Chinese cabbage is when it's braised or stewed until it's almost creamy. The sweetness and tenderness come through. I might add a bundle of bean thread noodles, too, to make it even better. This cabbage dish and a bowl of rice ground me in simplicity.

■ In a medium pot over high heat, combine the cabbage and water, and bring to a boil, then reduce heat to low. It may not look like there's enough water, but the cabbage cooks down substantially. Let simmer for about 15 minutes, stirring occasionally. Add the soy sauce and shallots and let simmer for another 15 minutes, stirring occasionally. If adding the bean thread, add it about 5 minutes before taking the soup off the heat. (The noodles will absorb a bit of the broth, so you can add about ½ cup water, if needed, to loosen up the mixture.) Taste the broth. Add the kosher salt to taste and the white pepper powder. Stir to combine and taste again. Adjust as needed. If desired, you can garnish with extra fried shallots. Serve while hot.

Mian Pian Soup

MAKES 4 SERVINGS

1 teaspoon vegetable oil

2 cups sliced baby bok choy or Chinese cabbage, about ½-inch pieces

1 stalk green onion, finely chopped

¼ cup thinly shaved carrot coins

6 cups Ginger-Red Date Broth (page 110)

1 to 1½ teaspoons kosher salt, or to taste

15 wonton wrappers, cut in half

½ teaspoon sesame oil

⅛ teaspoon white pepper powder

Chili oil or chili sauce, for garnish (optional)

Chopped fresh cilantro, for garnish (optional)

There are not enough words in English for noodles. *Mian* (noodle) *pian* (pieces or sheet) is a casual noodle that doesn't have a set shape and usually ends up in soups. It was always at my father's request that my mother would make it for the family. She would use premade wonton wrappers and chicken broth or a quick vegetable broth. Like any noodle soup, it makes you feel like you're wrapped in a giant, fuzzy blanket. Nowadays, if I make wontons and have a few extra wrappers, I'll make my mother a bowl of mian pian soup as a nod to the old days.

■　In a medium pot, heat the vegetable oil over medium-high heat. Add the baby bok choy or cabbage and stir, cooking 1 to 2 minutes, or until softened. Add the onion and carrots and stir to combine. Add the broth and salt, raise the temperature to high, and bring to a boil. Reduce the heat to low and let simmer.

■　Separate the wonton wrappers and drop them one piece at a time into the broth, stirring occasionally so they get submerged in the broth and don't stick to each other. Let cook for 1 to 2 minutes, or until the noodles have gone from a dull, pasty look to a glistening, slippery look. Add the sesame oil and white pepper powder. Garnish with chili oil or chili sauce and cilantro.

Hot-and-Sour Soup

with Dried Lily Flowers

MAKES 4 SERVINGS

6 cups Vegetable Broth (page 109)

¼ cup soy sauce, plus more as needed

¼ cup white vinegar, plus more as needed

2 teaspoons white pepper powder, plus more as needed

1 (14-ounce) block medium or firm tofu

¼ cup wood ear mushrooms, soaked in warm water for 20 minutes and thinly sliced

6 medium dried shiitake mushrooms, soaked in hot tap water for 2 to 3 hours, stemmed, and thinly sliced

¼ cup dried lily flowers, soaked in warm water for 30 minutes and hard tips trimmed

About 1 cup bamboo shoot strips (canned is fine)

⅓ cup cornstarch mixed with ½ cup water to make a slurry

3 large eggs, beaten

1 teaspoon sesame oil

Finely chopped green onions, for garnish (optional)

Chopped fresh cilantro, for garnish (optional)

Chili oil, for garnish (optional)

Hot-and-sour soup is a restaurant workhorse that has crossed into the mainstream. You can find recipes for it via any number of food-related sites. I have a long history with hot-and-sour soup because it was one of my responsibilities to make vats of this soup for my family's restaurant. For a long time, I couldn't get the balance of the flavors just right for a family-size portion because I only knew how to make it for one hundred. This version calls for dried lily flowers. If you can't get to an Asian market to buy them or find them online, you can leave them out.

■ In a medium pot, combine the broth, soy sauce, white vinegar, and white pepper powder and bring to a boil. Meanwhile, cut the tofu block in half, then cut into ¼ inch-thick slices. The slices will naturally shingle. Julienne the tofu so that you get fine strips. Repeat with the other half. Add the tofu, wood ear, shiitake, lily flowers, and bamboo shoots to the broth. Stir. When the mixture comes to a boil, reduce the heat to medium low and let simmer for 2 to 3 minutes.

■ Slowly swirl in the cornstarch slurry as you stir the soup with a spoon. Continue stirring a few times to integrate the starch and thicken the soup. When the soup starts to bubble again, pour the beaten eggs in a steady, circular stream to create threads of egg. The eggs will blossom in the soup. Stir to break up the eggs. Taste for seasoning. If needed, add more soy sauce, vinegar, and white pepper powder. Finish with the sesame oil. If using the garnishes, you can either add them to the pot or you can portion the soup into individual bowls and add the garnishes then.

紅燒蘿蔔

Braised Daikon

MAKES 4 SERVINGS

1 pound daikon, peeled and cut into 2-inch chunks

4 cups water

8 dried Chinese red dates

4 medium dried shiitake mushrooms

1 stalk green onion, cut into 3-inch-long segments

2 tablespoons soy sauce

¼ teaspoon kosher salt, if needed

Suggested pairings: Lucky 8 Stir-Fry (page 154) and Eggplant with Black Bean Garlic Sauce (page 170)

Daikon can be pungent, but this method tones down that pepperiness. The addition of dried red dates provides a sweet counterpoint—and you can eat the dates, which will be soft and creamy after all that braising. Usually, you need to soak the dried mushrooms, but, since the mushrooms braise for a while, you can skip that step. If you have leftover daikon and broth, you can add some more water, salt, and cooked noodles to it for an easy breakfast or lunch.

■ In a medium pot, combine the daikon, water, dates, mushrooms, onion, and soy sauce. Bring to a boil over high heat, then reduce the heat to low and let simmer for 35 to 45 minutes, stirring occasionally, until the daikon is tender and translucent. Taste the broth and, if needed, add salt. Serve while hot.

Chinese Purple Seaweed and Tofu Soup

MAKES 4 SMALL SERVINGS

3 cups Vegetable Broth (page 109)

About 7 ounces tofu, cut into ½-inch cubes

1 cup purple seaweed, cut with scissors roughly into 2-inch pieces

½ teaspoon kosher salt

1 egg, beaten

¼ teaspoon sesame oil

This is my mother's breakfast soup, which comes together in a snap. Chinese purple seaweed (or *zicai: zi* is purple and *cai* is vegetable) is, indeed, purple, though it looks black in the package. It's usually sold in a large disc that you break apart into the amount you need. If you don't have vegetable broth, you can use water.

■　In a medium pot, combine the broth and tofu. Bring to a boil, then reduce the heat to medium low. Add the seaweed and salt, stirring to combine. Let simmer for 1 to 2 minutes.

■　Drizzle in the beaten egg and immediately stir so the ribbons of egg don't become a big clump. Let the soup come back to a simmer. Drizzle on the oil and give the soup one last stir before serving.

Rice Cake Soup

with Vegetables

MAKES 4 SERVINGS

1 teaspoon vegetable oil

2 to 3 cups baby spinach

1 stalk green onion, finely chopped

½ cup fresh mushrooms, such as beech or enoki

¼ cup thinly shaved carrot coins

6 cups Ginger-Red Date Broth (page 110)

1½ teaspoons kosher salt, or to taste

1½ cups sliced rice cake

½ teaspoon sesame oil

⅛ teaspoon white pepper powder

Chopped fresh cilantro, for garnish (optional)

Rice cake is made of rice but can behave like a noodle, which means it's the best of both worlds. You can use baton- or pearl-shaped rice cake too. I usually buy a large pack of sliced rice cake and freeze whatever I don't use. Feel free to try different vegetables according to your taste. You can serve this as part of a larger meal or on its own.

▪ In a medium pot, heat the vegetable oil over medium-high heat. Add the spinach, onion, mushrooms, and carrots, and stir to combine. Add the broth and salt, raise the temperature to high, and bring to a boil. Reduce the heat to medium low.

▪ Add the rice cake slices, stir, and let simmer for 5 to 7 minutes, or until soft. Check occasionally for the doneness of the rice cake. Carefully take a bite of a piece. If it's soft and you can bite through it easily, it's done. You don't want to overcook it or it will turn mushy. Add the sesame oil and white pepper powder. Top with cilantro.

Vegetarian Wonton Soup

MAKES 4 SERVINGS

For the wontons:

About 7 ounces firm tofu, cut into ½-inch cubes

2 cups roughly chopped Chinese cabbage

½ cup chopped pickled Chinese mustard greens (optional)

2 stalks green onions, roughly chopped

6 medium dried shiitake mushrooms, soaked in hot water for 2 to 3 hours, stemmed, and roughly diced

1 bundle bean thread noodles, soaked in warm water for 10 minutes and roughly chopped

2 tablespoons soy sauce

⅛ teaspoon white pepper powder

1 teaspoon sesame oil

1 (14-ounce) pack wonton wrappers

8 cups water

For the soup:

6 cups Ginger-Red Date Broth (page 110)

1 to 1½ teaspoons kosher salt, or to taste

Finely chopped fresh cilantro, for garnish

Green onions, for garnish

Wonton soup is beloved. It's accessible, satisfying, and soothing. While this recipe suggests six to eight wontons per person, you certainly could add more. The recipe yields enough to offer everyone a few extras. I find that once you start eating the soup, eight wontons disappear too quickly. Normally, when I make chicken wontons, I will add some leaves of baby bok choy to the broth. Since these wontons have a vegetable filling, I skipped adding extra greens.

▪ To make the wontons, combine the tofu, cabbage, mustard greens, onions, mushrooms, bean thread, soy sauce, white pepper powder, and oil in the bowl of a food processor. Pulse together until blended, but don't let it become paste.

▪ Place just less than 1 teaspoon of the filling at the center of the wonton wrapper. You will have to adjust the amount of filling as needed because wonton wrappers can vary in dimension. Fill a small bowl with about ¼ cup water. Dip your finger into the water and moisten the edges of the wrapper. Fold the wrapper in half over the filling, line up the edges, and press down to flatten and seal. You will now have a rectangular packet. Carefully bend the rectangle so that the two bottom corners meet—kind of like a fortune cookie—and overlap the corners, sealing with a dab of water. Repeat with the remaining wrappers and filling. Place the finished wontons on a parchment-lined baking sheet. You will need 6 to 8 wontons per person. (Any extra wontons can be frozen, but don't defrost them or they will be a mess. Frozen wontons are best boiled.)

▪ Bring the 8 cups water to a boil in a large pot over high heat.

▪ To make the soup, bring the Ginger-Red Date Broth to a boil in a separate large pot. Reduce the heat to low to keep warm. Season the broth with salt.

▪ When the water comes to a boil, add the wontons. Cook for 2 to 3 minutes, or until the wrappers lose their opaqueness and start to glisten. Drain or use a large slotted spoon or strainer to transfer the cooked wontons to the broth. Let simmer for about 1 minute. Ladle the wontons into bowls with some broth. Top with cilantro and green onions.

▪ To make wontons in chili sauce, boil the wontons as directed, and serve with the Chili Sauce (recipe follows). →

Chili Sauce

½ cup Chili Oil (page 207)

2 stalks green onions, finely minced

2 teaspoons finely minced garlic

1 teaspoon sugar

1 teaspoon sesame oil

½ cup soy sauce

2 tablespoons balsamic vinegar

You can easily make wontons in chili sauce. Make and boil the wontons as instructed in the Vegetarian Wonton Soup recipe. Instead of making the broth, use this sauce.

■ In a medium bowl, combine the chili oil, onions, garlic, sugar, sesame oil, soy sauce, and vinegar. Stir to combine. This will keep in an airtight jar in the refrigerator for several weeks.

Sweet Corn Soup

MAKES 4 SERVINGS

6 cups Ginger-Red Date Broth (page 110) or water (see Note)

3 cups fresh or frozen corn kernels

2 teaspoons kosher salt, or to taste, plus more as needed

¼ teaspoon white pepper powder

2 tablespoons cornstarch mixed with 2½ tablespoons water to make a slurry

2 large eggs, beaten

2 stalks green onions, finely chopped

2 teaspoons unseasoned rice vinegar (optional)

½ teaspoon sesame oil

If you keep a couple bags of frozen corn in the freezer, you'll always have one great soup in your back pocket. This soup is delicately hearty—yes, that's possible! While this version is meatless, I do make corn soup with chicken or, when in season, fresh Dungeness crab. I tend to keep the ingredients streamlined, but you certainly could add other vegetables to this and make it your own. If you are short on time, you can skip the blender step. Also, I like to finish with extra white pepper powder and chopped cilantro. So, feel free to adjust the seasonings to your liking.

▪ In a medium pot, combine the broth, corn, salt, and white pepper powder and bring to a boil over high heat. Reduce the heat to low and simmer for 5 minutes. Remove from heat. If you have an immersion blender, use it to blitz the soup in several 5-second pulses. Alternatively, blend about 2 cups of the broth and corn in a blender for about 10 seconds or so until the corn kernels have broken apart and then pour it back into the pot. The idea is to create some body in the soup while leaving the remaining corn kernels whole.

▪ Return the soup to medium-low heat. Swirl in the cornstarch slurry, then stir the soup well with a spoon to combine. Reduce the heat to low. Swirl in the beaten eggs, then stir the soup again. Add the onions and finish with the rice vinegar and oil. Taste for seasoning. If needed, add salt.

NOTE: If you use water, add ½ teaspoon grated fresh ginger to the liquid.

高麗菜番茄粉絲湯

Taiwanese Cabbage and Tomato Soup

with Bean Thread Noodles

MAKES 4 SERVINGS

1 teaspoon vegetable oil

½ cup diced fresh tomatoes

1 stalk green onion, finely chopped

6 cups Vegetable Broth (page 109) or water

2½ cups Taiwanese cabbage, cut into 1-inch squares

1 tablespoon soy sauce

½ teaspoon kosher salt

1 bundle bean thread noodles, soaked in warm water for 10 minutes

½ teaspoon sesame oil

⅛ teaspoon white pepper powder

Back in my family's restaurant days, we often ate our meals at odd hours and in a hurry. This soup is something that my mother would throw together with some meatballs. The Taiwanese cabbage (see page 142) gives it sweetness. But if you can't find Taiwanese cabbage, you can use regular green cabbage. In summer, when tomatoes are in season, use a juicy one. In the winter, I've had luck with greenhouse cherry tomatoes.

■ In a medium pot, heat the vegetable oil over high heat for a few seconds. Add the tomatoes and onion and stir for about 30 seconds. Add the broth or water, cabbage, soy sauce, and salt, and bring to a boil. Reduce the heat to low and let simmer for 10 minutes. Add the bean thread (but not the soaking water) and simmer for 5 minutes more. After the noodles start to soften, give it a stir. Finish with the sesame oil and white pepper powder.

Braised Bamboo Shoots and Shiitake Mushrooms

MAKES 4 SERVINGS

½ pound bamboo shoots, cut into 1-inch chunks

8 to 10 medium dried shiitake mushrooms, soaked in warm water for 2 to 3 hours to reconstitute and drained

1 large carrot, peeled and cut into ½-inch chunks on the bias

4 cups water, plus more as needed

¼ cup soy sauce, plus more as needed

1 teaspoon sugar

Suggested pairings: Yu Choy with Fried Shallots (page 132) and Winter Melon with Smoked Salt (page 169)

Braised bamboo shoots and shiitake mushrooms is a flavor combination that takes me back to moments in childhood. Bamboo shoots already have a distinct flavor that becomes extra savory when braised with mushrooms. It's hard to find fresh bamboo shoots in the United States. They're almost always canned or boiled and sold in markets in bins. If you can get whole chunks, then this would be a great dish to try.

- In a medium pot, combine the bamboo shoots, mushrooms, carrot, and the 4 cups water. Bring to a boil over high heat, then lower the heat to medium low. Add the soy sauce and sugar. Stir to combine. Let simmer for 20 to 30 minutes, uncovered, stirring occasionally. The broth will reduce, but you want to maintain the level of liquid to be at least half the level of the ingredients. Add water as needed. At about 20 minutes, taste for seasoning. If the liquid needs some salt, add a teaspoon of soy sauce, or to taste. Let simmer for 5 minutes more, then serve.

炒菜類

Stir-Fries

Garlic Yam Leaf 131

Yu Choy with Fried Shallots 132

Crisp Vegetables with Lily Flowers 135

Ginger-Scallion Pea Shoots 137

"BLT" (Beech Mushrooms, Lettuce, and Tomato) 138

Wok-Seared Edamame and Corn 141

Taiwanese Cabbage with Garlic and Chili 142

Dry-Fried Brussels Sprouts 144

Chinese Mustard Greens with Shishito Peppers 147

Gai Lan with Oyster Mushrooms 148

Hot-and-Sour Celery, Carrots, and Bean Sprouts 150

Cauliflower Rice with Eggplant and Gai Lan 151

Shen's Wok-Seared Broccoli with Jalapeños 152

Lucky 8 Stir-Fry 154

When it comes to stir-fried vegetable dishes, I sometimes wonder whether formal recipes are necessary. Many vegetables combine well with any number of other vegetables, so there isn't a high risk of mismatches. The prep work is straightforward: Cut the vegetables into similar, bite-size pieces. Then, follow the basic procedure for a stir-fry: Heat oil in a wok over high heat, add ingredients, stir-fry for a minute, add sauce, stir-fry for a minute, serve. Of course that's an oversimplification, but the essential technique is the same across the landscape of ingredients.

Then I remind myself that there are nuances that need the space of a recipe to impart wisdom. I can apply the flavors of dry-fried green beans to Brussels sprouts, but how you trim green beans is very different from how you prepare Brussels sprouts. How a pound of *gai lan*, with its hearty leaves and thick stems, reacts to a hot wok is not the same as how a pound of tender yu choy surrenders to the heat, shrinking to a fraction of itself. There is so much to learn about how vegetables behave. Stir-fries can guide your exploration of vegetable harmonies.

I'm a broken record about how much I count on stir-fries during the week because I can quickly put a meal on the table that has enough variety to please everyone. While my family does eat meat, vegetables always complete the menu. When I open the refrigerator to decide what to cook for dinner, I always start with the produce bin. A leafy green or Chinese cabbage inevitably is the first to land on the cutting board. Then I figure out what secondary ingredients will pair well with the greens and what flavors the sauce might want.

As you dive into this chapter, consider getting a proper wok (page 54) if you don't have one. I'm generally relaxed about the specific equipment home cooks use because I'm more interested in minimizing the barriers to getting people to cook. But, for making great stir-fried vegetables, you want the best tool to help you strike the right balance of flavors and textures. Plus, the deep sides of the wok will help you corral those leafy greens that are tempted to escape during cooking.

蒜香番薯葉

Garlic Yam Leaf

MAKES 4 SERVINGS

1 pound yam leaves, rinsed

1 tablespoon vegetable oil

2 to 3 cloves garlic, crushed or finely minced

1 tablespoon water

1 teaspoon soy sauce

⅛ teaspoon white pepper powder

¼ teaspoon sesame oil

Suggested pairings: Simple Vegetable Fried Rice (page 193) and Spiced Tofu with Leeks and Cabbage (page 203)

Yam leaves are usually found only in Asian markets and are sold in large, sometimes unruly bunches. They're known for containing antioxidants and anti-inflammatory properties. Freshness is essential, so look for the brightest green leaves and stems you can find, and plan on cooking them within a day or two. The flavor of the leaves can be earthy, which works well with pungent garlic. Like any other leafy green, a pile of yam leaves cooks down to "nothing." But a little can go a long way. If you can't find yam leaf, you could do this recipe with spinach.

■ Pick the yam leaves and their tender stems from the core stem, which can be quite woody. Discard or compost the stems. Set the leaves aside.

■ Preheat a wok over high heat until wisps of smoke rise from the surface. Add the vegetable oil and heat for a few seconds until the surface starts to shimmer. Add the garlic and immediately stir for several seconds. Add the yam leaves and stir-fry for about 30 seconds. Add the water and soy sauce. Stir-fry for about 1 minute, or until the leaves have turned a rich, dark green. Turn off the heat. Add the white pepper powder and sesame oil. Give the greens one last stir and serve.

紅 蔥 酥 炒 油 菜

Yu Choy

with Fried Shallots

MAKES 4 SERVINGS

For the fried shallots:

3 tablespoons vegetable oil

1 medium shallot, peeled and thinly sliced

¼ teaspoon kosher salt

For the yu choy:

1 pound yu choy, trimmed and cut into ½-inch segments

2 tablespoons vegetable broth or water

1½ teaspoons soy sauce

⅛ teaspoon white pepper powder

Suggested pairings: Kung Pao Tofu Puffs (page 199) and Eggplant with Black Bean Garlic Sauce (page 170)

Yu choy is one of my go-to greens. It's more tender than *gai lan* (Chinese broccoli) but heartier than spinach. To trim, cut about a half inch of the stem end to remove any dried, fibrous bits. The rest of the stem is perfectly fine to eat. Some Asian markets sell yu choy *mui* (baby yu choy), which is even more tender. While you can use store-bought fried shallots to save a few minutes, you can't beat the flavor of freshly fried shallots.

■   Preheat a wok over medium heat until wisps of smoke rise from the surface.

■   To make the fried shallots, add the oil and heat until it starts to shimmer. Add the shallots and stir with the wok spatula to loosen the shallot rings. Let fry for 1 to 2 minutes, stirring frequently to ensure even browning. When the shallots are golden, turn off the heat. Using a slotted spoon, remove the shallots to drain on a paper towel–lined plate. Sprinkle with the salt. Set aside while you prepare the yu choy.

■   If there are any burnt bits left in the residual oil that's in the wok, carefully remove them with the spatula. Turn the heat to high and heat the oil for a few seconds until it starts to shimmer. Add the yu choy and stir-fry for 1 minute. Add the broth or water and the soy sauce. Stir-fry for 1 minute more. Add the fried shallots and stir to combine. Turn off the heat. Add the white pepper powder, stir again, and serve in a bowl.

How to Add Meat or Seafood

If you do eat meat or seafood, you can add your choice of protein based on the following sample methods.

CHICKEN: Cut about 8 ounces chicken breast lengthwise into two to three strips, about 1½ inches wide, or about the size of chicken tenders. Then slice each strip of chicken crosswise into slivers. The exact size of the slivers is not as important as keeping the pieces relatively uniform. Similarly, you can cut chicken thighs into slivers. In a small bowl, combine the chicken with 1 tablespoon soy sauce and mix well. Add 2 teaspoons cornstarch and mix well again. Preheat a wok over high heat until wisps of smoke rise from the surface. Add 2 tablespoons vegetable oil and heat until it shimmers. Add the chicken and, using a spatula, quickly spread it into a single layer in the bowl of the wok. After about 15 seconds, stir-fry the chicken for 1 minute more, or until the chicken is nearly cooked through. Remove the wok from the heat, transfer the chicken to a small bowl, and set aside. Choose the vegetable dish to which you'd like to add the chicken, adding it before you add the sauce ingredients.

BEEF: Trim about ½ pound flank steak of any large pieces of membrane. Cut the flank in half or thirds lengthwise or with the grain. Depending on the total width of the flank, you may get two or three sections that are about 3 inches wide. Cut these sections against the grain into ⅛-inch-thick slices. Place the beef in a medium bowl. Add 1 tablespoon soy sauce and mix well. Add 2 teaspoons cornstarch and mix well again. Preheat a wok over high heat until wisps of smoke rise from the surface. Add 1 tablespoon vegetable oil and heat until it starts to shimmer. Gently add the beef and, using a spatula, quickly spread it into a single layer in the bowl of the wok. Sear the beef for about 15 seconds and then stir-fry for 1 to 2 minutes, breaking up any pieces that have stuck together. Remove the wok from the heat, transfer the beef to a medium bowl, and set aside. Rinse the wok and dry with a towel. Choose the vegetable dish to which you'd like to add the beef, adding it before you add the sauce ingredients.

PORK: Trim the fat off about 8 ounces thin-cut pork loin chop. Cut the chop lengthwise into two to three strips, about 1 inch wide, or about the size of chicken tenders. Then slice each strip of pork crosswise into slivers. Remember, the size of the slivers is not as important as keeping the pieces relatively uniform. In a small bowl, combine the pork with 1 tablespoon soy sauce and mix well. Add 2 teaspoons cornstarch and mix well again. Preheat a wok over high heat until wisps of smoke rise from the surface. Add 2 tablespoons vegetable oil and heat until it shimmers. Add the pork and, using a wok spatula, quickly spread it into a single layer in the bowl of the wok. After about 15 seconds, stir-fry the pork for 1 minute more, or until the pork is nearly cooked through. Remove the wok from the heat, transfer the pork to a small bowl, and set aside. Choose the vegetable dish to which you'd like to add the pork, adding it before you add the sauce ingredients.

SHRIMP: Peel and devein about ½ pound shrimp. In a small bowl, put the shrimp and 1 tablespoon soy sauce and mix well. Add 2 teaspoons cornstarch and mix well again. Set aside. Preheat a wok over high heat until wisps of smoke rise from the surface. Add 1 tablespoon vegetable oil and heat until it starts to shimmer. Add the shrimp in a single layer to the bowl of the wok and sear for 30 to 40 seconds, or until the shrimp have begun to turn pink. Flip the shrimp and sear for 30 to 40 seconds more. Remove the pan from the heat, transfer the shrimp to a small bowl, and set aside.

脆葉炒金針

Crisp Vegetables

with Lily Flowers

MAKES 4 SERVINGS

1 tablespoon vegetable oil

2 stalks green onions, trimmed and thinly sliced on the bias

2 cloves garlic, finely chopped

1 small yellow or orange bell pepper, seeded and very thinly sliced (or 4 mini sweet peppers, seeded and thinly sliced)

1 cup sliced pickled Chinese mustard greens

½ cup loosely packed dried lily flowers, soaked in warm tap water for 30 minutes and trimmed of hard tips

1 cup reconstituted dried wood ear mushrooms, roughly chopped into 1-inch pieces

1 tablespoon soy sauce

¼ teaspoon white pepper powder

Suggested pairing: Simply Steamed Baby Bok Choy (page 160)

This is one of those dishes that feels inventive because it was the result of ingredients thrown together. But it's based on core principles of Chinese cooking: balancing flavors and textures. Sweetness from the bell peppers, acidity from the pickles, crunch from the wood ear, and slight chewiness from the lily flowers. It's new and familiar all at once.

■ Preheat a wok over high heat until wisps of smoke rise from the surface. Swirl in the oil and heat until it starts to shimmer. Add the onions and stir-fry for 10 seconds to release the aroma. Add the garlic, bell peppers, and mustard greens. Stir-fry for about 1 minute. Drain the lily flowers and add to the wok. Add the wood ear and stir-fry to combine. Add the soy sauce and stir-fry for 1 to 2 minutes more until all the ingredients and the sauce have had a chance to mingle. Finish with a sprinkling of white pepper powder, and give it one last stir. Serve with rice. This would also taste good at room temperature as a side or appetizer.

蔥薑豌豆苗

Ginger-Scallion Pea Shoots

MAKES 4 SERVINGS

1 tablespoon vegetable oil

1 stalk green onion, finely chopped

1 large clove garlic, crushed or minced

1 teaspoon minced or grated fresh ginger

¾ pound pea shoots, leaves separated and stems roughly chopped

¾ teaspoon kosher salt

1 to 2 tablespoons water

Suggested pairing: Fried Brown Rice with Oyster Mushrooms and Greens (page 180)

I didn't learn to love anything related to fresh peas until I was an adult. I think it was because we had only frozen peas growing up and the flavor and texture weren't appealing. When I first tasted freshly shelled peas, it was a revelation. Only then did I become open to trying pea shoots. Especially when stir-fried in hot oil in a wok, pea shoots speak a language of their own. Not all pea shoots are equal in tenderness, though. While the leaves and tendrils tend to be delicate, the stems can sometimes be fibrous. Be sure to give them a rough chop before cooking. Also note that the terms "pea shoots" and "pea sprouts" are sometimes used interchangeably and that micro pea shoots/sprouts can also be used in this recipe.

■ Preheat a wok over medium heat until wisps of smoke rise from the surface. Add the oil, onion, garlic, and ginger. Stir for about 10 seconds. Add the pea shoots, turn up the heat to high, and stir-fry for about 1 minute. Add the salt and water. Stir-fry for 1 minute, or until the pea shoots look dark green and are cooked through but not soggy. Serve while hot.

鴻喜菇，生菜，番茄

"BLT"

(Beech Mushrooms, Lettuce, and Tomato)

MAKES 4 SERVINGS

1 tablespoon vegetable oil

1 medium beefsteak or 2 Roma tomatoes, cut into 1-inch chunks; or 1½ cups cherry tomatoes, halved

1 tablespoon black bean garlic sauce

1 tablespoon soy sauce

1 tablespoon water

2 stalks green onions, finely chopped

4 ounces beech (also called *bunashimeji*) mushrooms, trimmed and gently separated

1 head romaine lettuce or other hearty variety, halved, cored, and cut into 2-inch segments

⅛ teaspoon white pepper powder

Suggested pairings: Sweet Potatoes with Chili-Shallot Jam (page 174) and Tofu, Peas, and Carrots (page 212)

To be honest, I prefer to make this dish with bacon. But that doesn't mean stir-fried lettuce isn't delicious without bacon. I was skeptical the first time I heard about stir-fried lettuce, but once I tasted it, it made sense. It is a leafy green, after all. Black bean garlic sauce gives this dish some punch. Use a hearty lettuce, such as romaine or green or red leaf. If you have access to a well-stocked Chinese market, you can use Taiwanese lettuce, which resembles an elongated romaine lettuce. Get juicy, ripe tomatoes—any variety—that burst with flavor. If you can't find beech mushrooms, use shiitake or oyster mushrooms.

■ Preheat a wok over high heat until wisps of smoke rise from the surface. Add 1 tablespoon oil and heat until it starts to shimmer. Add the tomatoes and stir-fry for 20 to 30 seconds to release the juices. Add the black bean garlic sauce, soy sauce, water, and onions. Stir to combine and let simmer for about 30 seconds. Add the mushrooms and lettuce and stir-fry briskly for 1 to 2 minutes to wilt the leaves and coat with sauce. Add the white pepper powder and stir. Transfer to a serving dish.

毛豆炒玉米

Wok-Seared Edamame and Corn

MAKES 4 SERVINGS

2 ears fresh corn or 1 (10-ounce) bag frozen corn

1 tablespoon vegetable oil

2 stalks green onions, finely chopped

1 cup shelled edamame (frozen is fine)

1 tablespoon soy sauce

1 tablespoon water

Kosher salt (optional)

Suggested pairing: Asparagus with Shiitake and Oyster Mushrooms (page 163)

If you keep bags of frozen corn and frozen shelled edamame stocked, this can be a "sure thing" dish when you're short on time. The technique is straightforward and the wok-searing imparts great flavor. While the recipe is intended for a wok, you could put this together in a cast-iron skillet too. Instead of edamame, you could use peas.

■   If using fresh corn, cut the kernels from the cob. Set aside.

■   Preheat a wok over high heat until wisps of smoke rise from the surface. Add the oil and onions, and quickly stir to combine for 10 seconds, or until the onions are fragrant.

■   Add the corn and edamame, and stir-fry for about 1 minute. It will sizzle as the frozen vegetables cook through.

■   Add the soy sauce and water, and continue to stir. After 1 to 2 minutes more, the corn should have a light sear and be fully cooked through. If needed, add salt to taste. Serve with steamed rice.

辣炒蒜香高麗菜

Taiwanese Cabbage
with Garlic and Chili

MAKES 4 SERVINGS

About 1 pound Taiwanese cabbage (usually about a quarter of a large head or, when cut, roughly 6 cups packed)

½ teaspoon kosher salt

1 tablespoon vegetable oil

1 red chili pepper, such as aji, cayenne, or bird, depending on your spice tolerance, sliced ¼ inch thick

1 to 2 cloves garlic, crushed or minced

1 tablespoon soy sauce

1 tablespoon water

Suggested pairings: Meatless Ma Po Tofu (page 206) and Gai Lan with Oyster Mushrooms (page 148)

Also known as flat cabbage, Taiwanese cabbage has a squat shape. A full head may weigh several pounds. Asian markets often sell them cut in half or quarters. The taste is mild and slightly sweet. Salting the leaves first helps to break down the fibers before stir-frying—though you can skip this step if you're in a hurry. An alternative flavor profile might include ¼ to ½ teaspoon freshly cracked Sichuan peppercorns, 1 teaspoon chili oil, or 1 teaspoon unseasoned rice vinegar. If you can't find Taiwanese cabbage, you can use Chinese (napa) cabbage or regular green cabbage.

■ Cut out the core from the wedge of cabbage. The easiest way to do this is to set the cabbage on one of the flat sides with the core end facing toward you. Make a cut through the cabbage at an angle around the core. Then, cut the cabbage into roughly 1-inch-square pieces and place in a large mixing bowl. Sprinkle the salt on the cabbage and work it into the leaves, squeezing fistfuls of cabbage at a time. Repeat this vigorously for about 1 minute. Set aside.

■ Preheat a wok over medium-high heat until wisps of smoke rise from the surface. Swirl the oil into the wok. Immediately add the chili pepper and garlic, and stir for about 5 seconds to keep from burning. Add the cabbage and stir-fry actively to mix with the aromatics, 1 to 2 minutes, or until you start to see some charred edges on the cabbage leaves. Add the soy sauce and water. Stir-fry for 1 to 2 minutes more, or until the cabbage has cooked through but isn't soggy. Serve with rice or noodles. This also pairs well with congee.

FUNNY STORY

My husband didn't "discover" Taiwanese cabbage until he went out to a Chinese restaurant with a buddy of his who ordered it. Even though my mother and I have been cooking and eating this dish for years, my husband never paid attention to it because he generally doesn't like cabbage. "Why don't you ever make Taiwanese cabbage?" he asked me after he came home from dinner. All I could do was shake my head.

乾煸球芽甘藍

Dry-Fried Brussels Sprouts

MAKES 4 SERVINGS

1 pound Brussels sprouts

2 tablespoons plus 1 teaspoon vegetable oil

2 tablespoons water, divided

2 stalks green onions, trimmed and finely chopped

1 tablespoon peeled and finely minced fresh ginger

2 cloves garlic, crushed or finely minced

4 medium or 6 small dried shiitake mushrooms, soaked in warm water for at least 1 hour to reconstitute, and cut into ¼-inch dice

1½ tablespoons soy sauce

1½ teaspoons sugar

Suggested pairings: Eggplant with Black Bean Garlic Sauce (page 170) and Seared Tofu with Baby Bok Choy (page 214)

Dry-fried green beans is a popular dish in many Chinese restaurants—and at home. When I make the green beans, I add a small amount of ground pork, which caramelizes with the aromatics to create flavorful bits that punctuate the beans. I wanted to apply the same technique to Brussels sprouts and use diced shiitake mushrooms instead of pork. The mushrooms already have a distinct flavor that only amplifies in this preparation. I like this dish with rice any night of the week, but it can also be a star side at, say, Thanksgiving dinner.

- To trim the Brussels sprouts, cut off the stem end and peel away any rough outer leaves. Set each sprout on the flat side and slice ¼ inch thick.

- Preheat a wok over high heat until wisps of smoke rise from the surface. Add the 2 tablespoons oil and heat for a few seconds until the oil shimmers. Add the Brussels sprouts and stir-fry briskly for 1 minute. Add 1 tablespoon of the water and continue to stir-fry for 2 minutes more, or until the edges of the sprouts start to char. Turn off the heat and scoop the sprouts into a medium bowl. Set aside while you make the sauce.

- Heat the remaining 1 teaspoon oil in the wok over medium heat for about 5 seconds. Add the onions, ginger, garlic, and mushrooms. Stir-fry for 10 seconds, or until the aromatics become fragrant. Add the Brussels sprouts and stir-fry for 30 seconds. Add the soy sauce, the remaining 1 tablespoon water, and sugar, and stir-fry actively for 1 to 2 minutes, or until the sauce caramelizes. This can happen pretty quickly, so pay attention. When the Brussels sprouts look sufficiently coated with the sauce and well combined with the aromatics, turn off the heat and transfer to a serving bowl.

NOTE: To make dry-fried green beans instead, use ¾ pound green beans, preferably the more tender haricots verts. Trim the green beans. Heat ⅓ cup vegetable oil in a wok over medium-high heat for 30 to 60 seconds, or until it starts to shimmer. In batches, add the beans to the oil in a single layer. Stir-fry the beans, gently swishing them around in the oil until the skins start to blister, 1 to 2 minutes. Use a slotted spoon and transfer the beans to a bowl. Repeat with the remaining beans. Clean out the wok, then proceed with instructions to make the sauce.

BRANCH OF BRUSSELS

In the fall, usually in October and especially around Thanksgiving, grocery stores and farmers' markets will sell whole branches of Brussels sprouts. You can't beat the freshness of Brussels sprouts still on the branch. While they look funky and intimidating, they're straightforward to handle. You can twist the sprouts off or use a paring knife to cut them off the branch. Then, place the sprouts in a large work bowl and cover with cold tap water. Swish around to clean the dirt and any insects that might be hiding in the leaves. It may take two rounds of rinsing to get the sprouts clean. Do this in batches, if you don't have a big enough bowl. Some of the outer leaves on the sprouts may break loose. These are perfectly good to cook too. Cut the sprouts according to the recipe.

糯米椒炒芥菜

Chinese Mustard Greens

with Shishito Peppers

MAKES 4 SERVINGS

1 tablespoon vegetable oil

¾ pound fresh Chinese mustard greens (*gai choy*) or ½ pound regular mustard greens

½ cup thinly sliced pickled Chinese mustard greens (can be store-bought) or 1 tablespoon rice vinegar (see Note)

¼ pound fresh shishito peppers (5 or 6), stemmed and sliced thinly on the bias (no need to remove the seeds)

1 tablespoon soy sauce

1 to 2 tablespoons water

¼ teaspoon white pepper powder

Suggested pairing: Sweet Potatoes with Chili-Shallot Jam (page 174)

I was cooking my feelings when I combined fresh bitter greens, acidic pickles, and shishito peppers—which are usually mild and can lull you into thinking that they don't have the capacity to hit you when you least expect it. Blistered shishito peppers with lemon juice and coarse salt became popular in restaurants and then markets began selling the peppers more widely. I wanted to do something besides blistering, and stir-frying is an obvious alternative. Adding a dash of white pepper powder at the end is a counterpoint for all the bitter-green notes.

■ Preheat a wok over high heat until wisps of smoke rise from the surface. Swirl in the oil and heat until it starts to shimmer. Add the fresh mustard greens and stir-fry for 30 seconds. Add the pickled mustard greens and shishito peppers, and stir-fry to combine. Add the soy sauce and water. Stir-fry for 1 to 2 minutes, or until all the ingredients are thoroughly combined and the greens have cooked down a bit. Sprinkle on the white pepper powder, and give the mixture one last stir. Turn off the heat and transfer to a serving dish.

NOTE: Instead of pickled Chinese mustard greens, you can add a mild vinegar for the acidity. I suppose you could use a bit of sauerkraut, though the caraway would add a different note to the dish.

Gai Lan

with Oyster Mushrooms

MAKES 4 SERVINGS

About ¾ pound *gai lan* (Chinese broccoli)

About ¼ pound oyster mushrooms

2 teaspoons soy sauce

1½ teaspoons hoisin sauce

2 tablespoons water

1 large clove garlic, crushed or minced

1 tablespoon vegetable oil

Suggested pairings: Winter Melon with Smoked Salt (page 169) and Spiced Tofu with Leeks and Cabbage (page 203)

Dim sum restaurants offer steamed whole *gai lan* stems drizzled with oyster sauce. I've always found them challenging to eat because Chinese restaurants don't include a knife as part of the place setting. So you're left gnawing on these stems that may be fibrous and not tender enough to be polite in taking a bite. The drizzle of oyster sauce packs a salty punch, but, for me, doesn't give the same satisfaction as vegetables cooked *with* a sauce. The heat of a wok is the magic flavor activator. In this vegetarian rendition, I skip the oyster sauce and use soy sauce and fresh garlic. Oyster mushrooms—or your choice of mushrooms—complement the crisp greens with earthiness and soft texture. Because cooking the mushrooms will cause a bit of smoke, make sure to turn the exhaust on high and/or open the window.

- Rinse and drain the *gai lan*, lightly shaking the excess water from the leaves into the sink. Trim about 1 inch off the thick end of the stem. Pluck or cut the leaves from the main stem and set aside. Peel the thick stems and slice thinly on the bias. (If you're feeling lazy, you can skip peeling.) Place the sliced stems in a medium bowl.

- Next, stack 4 or 5 leaves and make a lengthwise slice down the center of the stack of leaves. Stack the halves together and cut crosswise into 1-inch pieces. Add to the bowl and repeat with the next stack. Set aside. Separate the mushrooms into individual mushrooms and cut any larger ones into halves or thirds. In a small dip bowl or measuring cup, combine the soy sauce, hoisin, water, and garlic.

- Preheat a wok over high heat until wisps of smoke rise from the surface. Swirl in the oil and heat for a few seconds until it starts to shimmer. Add the mushrooms and stir-fry for 30 seconds to 1 minute, or until the edges start to brown. Add the *gai lan* and stir-fry for 1 minute, or until the color turns a rich green. Add the sauce mixture and combine well, stir-frying for about 1 minute to ensure the tangle of leaves get exposure to the sauce. Turn off the heat and transfer to a serving dish.

Hot-and-Sour Celery, Carrots, and Bean Sprouts

MAKES 4 SERVINGS

1 tablespoon vegetable oil

1 red chili pepper, such as Fresno, cut on the bias into ¼-inch-thick pieces

1 stalk celery, cut on the bias in ⅛-inch-thick slices

1½ cups loosely packed bean sprouts

½ cup dried wood ear mushrooms, soaked in warm water for 30 minutes and cut into ¼-inch-thick strips

1 medium carrot, cut into ¼-inch-thick strips

½ sweet bell pepper, cut into ⅛-inch-thick strips

1 tablespoon water

1 tablespoon soy sauce

1 teaspoon unseasoned rice vinegar or other mild vinegar

¼ teaspoon sesame oil

Suggested pairing: Fried Brown Rice with Oyster Mushrooms and Greens (page 180)

This is the kind of dish that might give you a new appreciation for celery, carrots, and bean sprouts. Celery and carrots, in particular, are workhorse vegetables, and we forget that they can be stars. You can scale up or down the amounts of a given vegetable to your taste. For example, the recipe calls for one rib of celery, but you could easily use two. If you're using the inner stalks of yellow celery hearts, which are progressively smaller, you will need several ribs. Because bean sprouts usually come in 9- to 12-ounce packages and are perishable, you will need to use them within a couple days of purchase. This recipe calls for only a portion of the sprouts. Other recipes that use bean sprouts include Vegetable Noodle Soup (page 191), Simple Vegetable Fried Rice (page 193), and Home-Style Egg Foo Yung with Curry Gravy (page 236).

■ Preheat a wok over high heat until wisps of smoke rise from the surface. Swirl in the vegetable oil and heat for a few seconds until it starts to shimmer. Add the chili pepper and stir-fry for about 5 seconds. Add the celery, bean sprouts, mushrooms, carrot, and bell pepper. Stir-fry for about 1 minute. Add the water and soy sauce. Stir-fry for about 1 minute. Drizzle on the rice vinegar and give it one good stir to combine. Turn off the heat, add the sesame oil, and transfer to a serving dish.

茄子芥藍炒花椰菜米

Cauliflower Rice

with Eggplant and Gai Lan

MAKES 4 SERVINGS

2 tablespoons vegetable oil

2 stalks green onions, finely chopped

1 to 2 cloves garlic, peeled and finely chopped

1 large Chinese eggplant, cut into roughly ½-inch dice (can leave the skin on)

2 cups cauliflower rice

2 hearty stalks *gai lan* (Chinese broccoli), trimmed and roughly chopped, about 1½ cups loosely packed

¼ cup water

1½ tablespoons fermented chili tofu (optional)

1 tablespoon soy sauce

¼ teaspoon kosher salt or to taste (optional)

Suggested pairing: Simple Stir-Fried Noodles (page 188)

Believe it or not, stir-fried cauliflower always felt like a treat to me when I was a kid. Since we ate most of our meals at my family's restaurant, we'd cook with the ingredients that we served on our menu. Because cauliflower was not a menu item, it would be something that my parents would buy from the grocery store when they got a craving. I don't understand cauliflower rice as a trendy replacement for rice, but bagged cauliflower rice is a great convenience product for a stir-fry any night of the week. With the addition of the fermented chili tofu, this dish has some funk.

■ Preheat a wok over high heat until wisps of smoke rise from the surface. Add the oil and heat until it starts to shimmer. Add the onions and stir-fry for 10 seconds. Stir in the garlic and add the eggplant. Stir-fry actively for about 2 minutes to let the heat soften the eggplant. Add the cauliflower rice and stir-fry for 1 to 2 minutes. Add the *gai lan* and stir-fry to combine.

■ Using the wok spatula, make a well in the middle of the mixture. Add the water, chili tofu, and soy sauce. Stir to combine and break down any larger chunks of the tofu. Then stir-fry with the cauliflower mixture to combine thoroughly. Turn off the heat. Taste for seasoning. It should be savory enough, but you can add salt to taste.

兒子深深的辣青花菜

Shen's Wok-Seared Broccoli
with Jalapeños

MAKES 4 SERVINGS

1 tablespoon vegetable oil

1 whole jalapeño pepper, cut into ¼-inch coins

1 to 2 cloves garlic, minced or crushed; or 1 teaspoon black bean garlic sauce

¾ pound broccoli crowns, cut into bite-size florets

3 tablespoons water

1 tablespoon soy sauce

Suggested pairings: Braised Chinese Cabbage with Fried Shallots (page 111) and Carrots and Celery with Spiced Tofu (page 204)

This is how I've eaten broccoli since I was a kid. I was not traumatized by overboiled, mushy florets. I'm tickled that my young son is now requesting broccoli stir-fried this way, so I promised to name this dish after him. You can use Broccolini or rapini in this preparation too. Be sure to cut the stems into 1-inch segments. Skip the peppers if you want to make this a mild dish.

■ Preheat a wok over high heat until wisps of smoke rise from the surface. Swirl in the oil and heat until it starts to shimmer. Add the jalapeño and garlic and stir-fry for 5 seconds. Add the broccoli and stir-fry for 2 minutes, or until the florets start to char on the edges. Add the water and soy sauce. Stir-fry for 1 to 2 minutes more, or until the broccoli has cooked through. The broccoli will still have some bite; it shouldn't be soggy. Turn off the heat and transfer to a serving dish.

Lunar New Year

Also called the Spring Festival, Lunar New Year falls sometime between January 20 and February 20. In some countries that celebrate the Lunar New Year, people and businesses typically get a two-week holiday break. The tradition—and expectation—is that those who live and work far from their hometowns and families will return to pay respects and celebrate the holiday. On New Year's Eve, people gather for the reunion feast to share copious amounts of foods imbued with symbolic wishes for health, wealth, prosperity, longevity, and good fortune.

The menu for the reunion feast must include a diversity of dishes from land and sea to represent abundance. For longevity, you serve long-life noodles or rice cake. For good luck, good fortune, prosperity, and wealth, you serve spring rolls, oysters, tangerines, kumquats, pomelo, whole fish, orange beef, dumplings (to eat at midnight), shrimp, and lobster. For abundance and family unity, you serve candies and seeds, lion's head meatballs, whole poultry, rice, and eggs. You will not leave hungry. And, in fact, the intent is to create leftovers so that there's no cooking or the use of a knife the next day lest you cut off the good fortune you garnered from the night before.

Children especially love the tradition of receiving red envelopes filled with money from elders. The red envelopes are meant as wishes for longevity. The money within is supposed to anchor many years of life for the recipient. For the holiday, everyone gets new clothes, and red is an auspicious color. All homes are cleaned to get rid of bad luck, and no sweeping is allowed in the first few days of the New Year or all the good luck will be swept away. Firecrackers are set off to scare away evil and bad fortune. Eight is the lucky number because the Chinese word for eight, *ba*, sounds like the word *fa* in *fa chai*—which means "get rich." In the United States, you can order special uncirculated dollar bills from the US Treasury that have a serial number starting with 8888. These bills are packaged beautifully in a clear sleeve and presented in a card that's designed to match a given year's corresponding zodiac animal. These bills sell out quickly every year before Lunar New Year. My mother orders one for each of her grandkids every year.

A cultural note: If you are invited to attend a Lunar New Year's dinner, a simple and meaningful gift for the host is a lovely bowl filled with tangerines, especially if they still have the leaves attached. Pre-Lunar New Year, Asian markets will stock tangerines with the leaves intact. It symbolizes good luck and good fortune, which is an appropriate sentiment. I have observed in recent years some failed attempts by supermarkets to acknowledge the holiday with floral arrangements or gift baskets that miss the mark. Notably, a high-end market made arrangements using Chinese take-out boxes that included a pair of chopsticks stabbed into the potting mixture. Aside from the box being crass, the protruding chopsticks represent death. Imagine showing up to a Chinese home with that as a gift! Stick with a round bowl (circles represent wholeness) filled with tangerines or a mix of tangerines and kumquats.

Here's a sample Lunar New Year menu featuring recipes in this book:

- Lucky 8 Stir-Fry (page 154)
- Simply Steamed Baby Bok Choy (page 160)
- Rice Cake Soup with Vegetables (page 118)
- Hong Kong–Style Crispy Noodles (page 194)
- Dad's Steamed Eggs with Tomatoes (page 228)
- Spring Rolls (page 92)
- Soup Dumplings (page 95)
- Gai Lan with Oyster Mushrooms (page 148)

發財熱炒

Lucky 8 Stir-Fry

MAKES 4 SERVINGS

1 tablespoon vegetable oil

1 cup bean sprouts

3 inner stalks celery hearts, cut on the bias ¼ inch thick

4 to 6 medium dried shiitake mushrooms, soaked in warm water for 2 to 3 hours

1 medium carrot, cut into ¼-inch-thick strips

½ cup dried lily flowers, soaked in warm water for 30 minutes

½ cup dried wood ear mushrooms, soaked in warm water for 30 minutes and cut into ¼-inch-thick strips

1 cup sliced Chinese cabbage or baby bok choy

8 snow peas, trimmed and cut on the bias into ½-inch-wide pieces

1 tablespoon soy sauce

1 tablespoon water

1 teaspoon Shaoxing wine, sherry, or dry Marsala wine

¼ teaspoon sesame oil

⅛ teaspoon white pepper powder

¼ teaspoon kosher salt (optional)

Suggested pairing: Simply Steamed Baby Bok Choy (page 160) and Gai Lan with Oyster Mushrooms (page 148)

Eight is a lucky number in the Chinese culture, especially at Lunar New Year. The Chinese word for "eight" is a homophone for prosperity, so numbers with consecutive eights in them represent "big money." This mixed vegetable dish takes its inspiration from Buddhist vegetarian cooking and can include any combination of ingredients that represent good luck, prosperity, happiness, family wholeness, and longevity. The ingredients also should have contrasting-yet-balanced flavors and textures. You can serve this on any day of the week—especially when it's Lunar New Year.

■ Preheat a wok over high heat until wisps of smoke rise from the surface. Swirl in the vegetable oil and heat for a few seconds until it starts to shimmer. Add all of the vegetables: bean sprouts, celery, shiitake mushrooms, carrot, dried lily flowers, wood ear mushrooms, Chinese cabbage or baby bok choy, and snow peas. Stir-fry for about 90 seconds and then add the soy sauce, water, and Shaoxing wine. Stir-fry for about 1 minute. Add the sesame oil and white pepper powder. Stir-fry for about 30 seconds more to combine. Turn off the heat. Taste for seasoning. If you think it needs a pinch of salt, add the kosher salt and stir to combine. Transfer to a serving dish.

蒸菜類

Steamed Dishes

Savory Mushrooms with Rice Powder 159

Simply Steamed Baby Bok Choy 160

Asparagus with Shiitake and Oyster Mushrooms 163

Gai Lan with Sesame Sauce 164

Cucumber and Wood Ear Mushrooms 165

Cauliflower with Edamame, Fried Onions, and Garlic 166

Winter Melon with Smoked Salt 169

Eggplant with Black Bean Garlic Sauce 170

Chinese Cabbage Heart with Goji Berries 173

Sweet Potatoes with Chili-Shallot Jam 174

For the Chinese, steaming is an essential cooking technique that highlights intrinsic flavors and produces beloved dishes that wouldn't otherwise exist. Buns and baozis, soup dumplings and *siu mai*, the entire contents of the dim sum cart, and so much more belong to the steamer. The pure flavor of steamed *gai lan*, Chinese cabbage, or any number of beautiful vegetables is satisfying and craveable. If cooking methods were personalities, stir-frying would be boisterous and impatient. Steaming would be calm and quietly confident.

But, steamed foods get a bad rap. The relative healthfulness of steamed vegetables makes it the go-to method for prescriptive meal plans, which connote deprivation from all that is flavorful. Need to go low-fat and low-salt? Eat some steamed vegetables! As a result of this association, people are programmed to react negatively to the idea of steamed foods. The benefits of steaming can't be denied. Notably, you don't need any oil (fat) to steam food—though you can *choose* to add, say, chili oil or sesame oil as a finishing touch. Also, the nutrients in the ingredients don't leach away in steaming as they do when you boil foods. But "steamed" shouldn't trigger an adverse reaction.

Many years ago, I read the book *Untangling My Chopsticks* by Victoria Riccardi, who had moved to Kyoto to study the art of kaiseki cooking. One of her observations, or revelations, was that she had to quiet down her mind and palate in order to taste the essence of the expertly prepared dishes she was experiencing. It required her to shift her Western mindset to better appreciate nuance and delicateness. This resonated with me.

In Chinese cooking, we have a term for foods that have a light flavor—*qing dan*—and it's not a euphemism for bland. It signifies that a dish is, indeed, delicately flavored and not heavy. It also implies the cook has thought about balancing a meal, so that strong flavors have a counterpoint. If you had only bold flavors in your meal, your palate would not get a break. While there are steamed dishes that are rich, many others possess that quality of *qing dan*. If a Chinese meal offers a spectrum of flavors and textures, then *qing dan* would be a key component of that scale.

粉蒸香菇

Savory Mushrooms

with Rice Powder

MAKES 4 SERVINGS

3 to 4 cups assorted mushrooms, such as shiitake, oyster, beech (*bunashimeji*), or trumpet

2 tablespoons soy sauce

1 tablespoon water

1 large clove garlic, crushed

1 green onion, finely chopped

1 packet (about 2 ounces) rice powder (see Note)

1 cauliflower steak (about ½ inch thick) or 1½ cups cauliflower florets (optional)

Suggested pairings: Yu Choy with Fried Shallots (page 132) and Taiwanese Cabbage with Garlic and Chili (page 142)

Traditionally, this dish is made with spare ribs. But rice powder (also known as steam powder), which is made of toasted and ground rice, works well with fresh mushrooms too. There are many more varieties of mushrooms available these days than ever, so don't hesitate to mix it up. For shiitakes, I prefer to use dried ones, which have a more concentrated flavor.

■ In a large bowl, combine the mushrooms with soy sauce, water, garlic, and onion. Mix well, making sure the marinade gets into the gills of the mushroom caps, and let marinate for about 10 minutes. In the meantime, set up a steamer and bring the water to a boil over high heat.

■ Sprinkle the rice powder over the mushrooms and toss well to coat. Place the cauliflower on a heatproof dish that fits in your steamer. Cover with the mushrooms, then place the dish in the steamer and cover. Steam for 30 minutes, or until the cauliflower is tender and the rice granules have plumped up. Serve while hot.

NOTE: A well-stocked Asian market will sell boxed rice powder. But different brands have different levels of five-spice seasoning and some can be overpowering. I grew up with the Taiwanese "white box" steam powder from Ruey Fah, which, lucky for me, is still available in some Chinese markets. For my taste, the seasoning is not too heavy-handed. You can make your own: In a dry skillet over medium-low heat, toast ½ cup long-grain rice (such as jasmine) for about 10 minutes, stirring continuously. After it's done toasting, set the rice aside to cool. Use a spice grinder to grind the rice into sesame-seed-size pellets. Be careful not to overgrind it. Add ¼ to ½ teaspoon five-spice powder to taste and mix well.

清蒸青江菜

Simply Steamed Baby Bok Choy

MAKES 4 SERVINGS

¾ pound baby bok choy, halved and cored

½ teaspoon kosher salt

Ginger-Scallion Oil (optional; recipe follows)

Suggested pairings: This could pair with almost anything because the flavor is mild.

Baby bok choy is relatively widely available and straightforward to cook. If possible, look for smaller heads of baby bok choy—about four inches or so—which can be steamed whole. If you have the larger ones, it will be necessary to separate the leaves from the core. You can keep the leaves whole or slice them into your desired width.

■ Set up a steamer and bring the water to a boil over high heat. Place the bok choy on a heatproof dish. If you have larger heads of bok choy, slice the leaves into ½-inch pieces before placing on the heatproof dish. Once the water is boiling, place the dish in the steamer, cover, and steam for 7 to 8 minutes for whole heads and 4 to 6 minutes for sliced. Season with salt. Serve with Ginger-Scallion Oil.

Ginger-Scallion Oil

MAKES ABOUT 1 CUP OIL

2½ cups finely chopped green onions

½ cup finely grated fresh ginger

¼ cup vegetable oil

1 teaspoon kosher salt

¾ teaspoon rice vinegar or Chinese black vinegar

You can use this as a condiment for steamed vegetables or with noodles. A rasp-style grater is best for the ginger.

■ In a medium bowl, combine the onions, ginger, oil, salt, and vinegar. Stir well to combine. Let rest, covered, on the counter for 30 to 60 minutes. This will keep in the refrigerator for several days.

TRIMMING BABY BOK CHOY

Cut about ¼ inch off the stem end of the bok choy. You can separate each leaf one-by-one from the stem by gently pulling it off. Or you can cut the bok choy in half lengthwise and then cut out the core.

You can rinse the leaves in cool water and drain. If you have a salad spinner, use it to dry the greens. If not, let the leaves rest in the colander for a few minutes to drain. Use according to the recipe.

蘆筍雙菇蒸

Asparagus
with Shiitake and Oyster Mushrooms

MAKES 4 SERVINGS

About 1 pound fresh asparagus, trimmed and cut into 1½-inch segments

8 small dried shiitake mushrooms, soaked in warm water for 30 minutes and halved

4 to 6 oyster mushrooms, larger pieces halved or quartered

¾ teaspoon kosher salt, plus more to taste

Suggested pairings: Sichuan Pepper Salt Fried Tofu (page 217) and steamed rice or Simple Vegetable Fried Rice (page 193)

This dish relies on the natural flavors of the ingredients, with just a bit of salt to enhance them. This combination would taste just as great in a stir-fry. If you'd like to give this steamed version a bit more punch, you can use the sauce for Cucumber and Wood Ear Mushrooms (page 165).

■ Set up a steamer and bring the water to a boil over high heat. Meanwhile, combine the asparagus, mushrooms, and salt in a medium bowl. Gently toss to combine. Place on a heatproof dish that fits in your steamer. Once the water is boiling, place the dish in the steamer, cover, and steam for 7 to 8 minutes, or until the asparagus and mushrooms have cooked through. Taste for seasoning. If you feel it needs a pinch more salt, add ⅛ teaspoon or to taste. Serve with rice or as a side dish.

芝麻醬蒸芥藍

Gai Lan

with Sesame Sauce

MAKES 4 SERVINGS

¾ pound *gai lan* (Chinese broccoli), stems sliced ¼ inch thick, leaves sliced 1 inch wide

1 tablespoon sesame paste

1 tablespoon soy sauce

½ teaspoon sugar

½ teaspoon grated ginger

1 large clove garlic, crushed

1 stalk green onion, finely chopped

1½ teaspoons balsamic vinegar

Suggested pairings: Sichuan Pepper Salt Fried Tofu (page 217), Vegetable Noodle Soup (page 191), or a selection of dim sum items

Steamed *gai lan* is delicious on its own, but it also can be a canvas for various sauces. In dim sum restaurants, *gai lan* is often served steamed or blanched and topped with oyster sauce. This sesame sauce hits all the flavor notes: salty with hints of sweet acid and garlic. Yu choy, bok choy, and other similar leafy greens would work well in this preparation.

■ Set up a steamer and bring the water to a boil over high heat. Place the *gai lan* on a heatproof dish that fits in your steamer. When the steamer is ready, place the dish in the steamer, cover, and steam for 5 to 6 minutes. In the meantime, in a small bowl, combine the sesame paste, soy sauce, sugar, ginger, garlic, onion, and vinegar. Serve the greens drizzled with the sauce or present the sauce on the side.

木耳小黃瓜

Cucumber and Wood Ear Mushrooms

MAKES 4 SERVINGS

4 Persian cucumbers, cut ¼ inch thick on the bias (about 1½ cups sliced)

20 small dried wood ear mushrooms, soaked in warm water for 20 minutes (about 1 cup reconstituted)

2 tablespoons soy sauce

1 tablespoon unseasoned rice vinegar

1 red chili pepper, such as serrano, seeded and finely diced

1 large clove garlic, crushed

1 stalk green onion, finely chopped

2 tablespoons vegetable broth or water

Suggested pairings: Chinese Mustard Greens with Shishito Peppers (page 147) or Lucky 8 Stir-Fry (page 154)

Usually relegated to salads or pickles, cucumbers can also star in cooked dishes. I prefer Persian or Japanese cucumbers because they don't need to be peeled. If you use another type, be sure to peel before cooking. The wood ear mushrooms add a contrasting texture. If you can't find the *yun er*-style small wood ear mushrooms (see page 20), then use the type available to you. Adjust the amount accordingly and, if necessary, cut larger pieces into quarter-size pieces.

■   Set up a steamer and bring the water to a boil over high heat. Meanwhile, combine the cucumbers and mushrooms in a shallow, heatproof bowl that fits in your steamer. Set aside. In a small bowl, combine the soy sauce, vinegar, chili, garlic, onion, and broth or water. Drizzle over the cucumber and mushroom mixture. Once the water is boiling, place the dish in the steamer, cover, and steam for 7 minutes, or until the cucumber slices are just cooked through. Serve while hot.

蒜香毛豆蒸白椰菜花

Cauliflower

with Edamame, Fried Onions, and Garlic

MAKES 4 SERVINGS

¾ to 1 pound cauliflower, cut into florets

½ cup frozen edamame

2 tablespoons vegetable oil

2 stalks green onions, finely chopped

2 large cloves garlic, finely chopped

¼ teaspoon kosher salt

⅛ teaspoon freshly ground Sichuan peppercorns

Suggested pairings: Fried Brown Rice with Oyster Mushrooms and Greens (page 180) and Dry-Fried Brussels Sprouts (page 144)

Let's have a moment of appreciation for cauliflower. You can use any variety or color for this dish. While the recipe calls for florets, you could use cauliflower steaks. The fried onions and garlic and the tingly Sichuan peppercorns offer a great punch.

■ Set up a steamer and bring the water to a boil over high heat. Place the cauliflower and edamame on a heatproof dish that fits in your steamer. Place the dish in the steamer, cover, and steam for 15 minutes, or until the florets are fork-tender.

■ Meanwhile, line a salad plate with a paper towel and set aside. Heat the oil in a small skillet over medium heat. When the surface of the oil shimmers, add the onions and garlic. Stir gently and fry until golden brown, 1 to 2 minutes. Using a spoon, carefully transfer the onions and garlic to the paper towel to drain. When the cauliflower is done, sprinkle on the onions and garlic. Finish with salt and Sichuan peppercorn.

清蒸冬瓜

Winter Melon

with Smoked Salt

MAKES 4 SERVINGS

About 1 pound winter melon

¼ cup water or vegetable broth

½ teaspoon smoked Maldon sea salt or other smoked sea salt

Suggested pairings: Garlic Yam Leaf (page 131) or Gai Lan with Oyster Mushrooms (page 148)

One of my favorite soups is winter melon with smoked ham hock, which is the inspiration for this delicate dish. Winter melon is a type of squash that's typically sold in Asian supermarkets and, because they can be quite large, are precut into manageable chunks. When selecting a portion of winter melon, make sure the flesh is firm, bright, and creamy white, and that the area around the seeds doesn't look rusted and mushy. Any extra winter melon can always be included in a stir-fry or soup.

■ Remove the seeds of the melon by carefully shimmying a knife under the seeds to cut them out. Place the melon flat side down, making sure it's stable. Then use a knife to shave off the peel. Be careful, because the peel is sturdy and you don't want your knife to slip. Once peeled, cut the melon into roughly 2-by-1-inch pieces that are ¼ inch thick.

■ Set up a steamer and bring the water to a boil over high heat. Meanwhile, place the melon slices in a shingled pattern on a heatproof dish that fits in your steamer. Add the water or broth. Once the water is boiling, place the dish in the steamer, cover, and steam for 10 minutes, or until tender. Remove from the heat. Before serving, sprinkle on the salt. This is best served hot with rice or as a side dish.

豆豉茄子

Eggplant
with Black Bean Garlic Sauce

MAKES 4 SERVINGS

¾ to 1 pound Chinese eggplant, trimmed and cut into 1-inch cubes

2 tablespoons black bean garlic sauce

1 tablespoon soy sauce

1 teaspoon water

1 stalk green onion, finely chopped

¼ teaspoon sesame oil

Suggested pairings: Simple Vegetable Fried Rice (page 193) and Crisp Vegetables with Lily Flowers (page 135)

While this can be made with any type of eggplant, I prefer the Chinese or Japanese varieties that have thinner skin you don't have to peel. If you use regular eggplant, be sure to shave off the skin with a sharp knife.

■ Set up a steamer and bring the water to a boil over high heat. Meanwhile, place the eggplant cubes in a heatproof dish that fits in your steamer. Set aside. In a small bowl, combine the black bean garlic sauce, soy sauce, water, onion, and oil. Once the water is boiling, place the dish of eggplant in the steamer basket. Cover with the lid and steam for about 10 minutes. Turn down the heat. Carefully remove the lid of the steamer. Drizzle the sauce over the eggplant, paying careful attention so that the steam doesn't burn your hand. Replace the lid and turn the heat back to high. Continue steaming for an additional 5 to 7 minutes, or until the eggplant is tender but not mushy. Before serving, gently toss the eggplant to combine with the sauce. This can be served hot or at room temperature.

构杞子蒸白菜心

Chinese Cabbage Heart

with Goji Berries

MAKES 4 SERVINGS

1 medium head Chinese cabbage

1 tablespoon goji berries

¼ teaspoon salt

Suggested pairings: Kung Pao Tofu Puffs (page 199) or Gai Lan with Oyster Mushrooms (page 148)

To have just the heart of the Chinese cabbage is a treat. The innermost golden leaves are the most tender and the sweetest. I love the presentation of the whole leaves, though it can be inelegant to eat them. Just before serving, you can slice across the mound of cabbage in half. The goji berries add a hint of sweetness—and purported health benefits.

■   Set up a steamer and bring the water to a boil over high heat. Meanwhile, cut the cabbage in half lengthwise through the core. Cut out the hard core of one of the halves. Remove about a 3-inch section of the cabbage heart, keeping the leaves intact. Reserve the outer leaves and remaining half of the cabbage for another meal. Place the "loaf" of cabbage cut side down on a heatproof dish. Sprinkle on the goji. Place the dish in the steamer, cover, and steam the cabbage for 20 to 25 minutes, or until the cabbage stems are translucent and tender. Sprinkle on the salt. You can serve the cabbage whole or, if preferred, you can cut the leaves in half crosswise. Serve with steamed rice.

紅蔥醬蒸番薯

Sweet Potatoes

with Chili-Shallot Jam

MAKES 4 SERVINGS

1 pound sweet potatoes, scrubbed, peeled, and cut into 1-inch chunks

½ cup Chili-Shallot Jam, or more as desired (recipe follows)

2 heaping tablespoons chopped fresh cilantro

Suggested pairings: Gai Lan with Oyster Mushrooms (page 148) or Ginger-Scallion Pea Shoots (page 137)

Sweet potatoes have so much flavor, you don't have to do much to them. In my family, my mother is the superfan and will eat roasted sweet potatoes unadorned or as an accompaniment to plain congee. When I served her this dish, she perked up and exclaimed, "This is good!" There's no higher compliment.

▪ Set up a steamer and bring the water to a boil over high heat. Meanwhile, place the sweet potatoes in a heatproof dish that fits in your steamer. Once the water is boiling, carefully place the dish in the steamer. Cover and steam over high heat for 15 minutes, or until the sweet potatoes are fork-tender. Turn off the heat and carefully remove the dish and set it on a plate or trivet. Spoon the jam over the sweet potatoes. Sprinkle with the cilantro and serve.

Chili-Shallot Jam

MAKES ABOUT 1 ½ CUPS

½ cup vegetable oil

3 cups thinly sliced shallots (about ¾ pound fresh shallots)

⅓ cup soy sauce

¼ cup sugar

1 tablespoon chili bean sauce, more or less to taste

This condiment can be used with stir-fried greens or any of the dumplings. If you prefer, you can make a mild version by skipping the chili bean sauce.

▪ Heat the oil in a small saucepan over medium heat until the surface of the oil starts to shimmer. Add the shallots and stir well to combine. Cook for about 1 minute, stirring a few times. Add the soy sauce, sugar, and chili bean sauce. Stir well to combine. Let the mixture come to a simmer and then turn the heat to low. Let the shallots cook down for 10 to 12 minutes, stirring frequently, until the shallots have become a dark caramel color. Turn off the heat and let the mixture cool, uncovered, in the pan for about 10 minutes. Use right away or transfer to a heatproof container or a glass jar, cover, and store in the refrigerator. Use within 3 weeks.

米飯麵條

Rice and Noodles

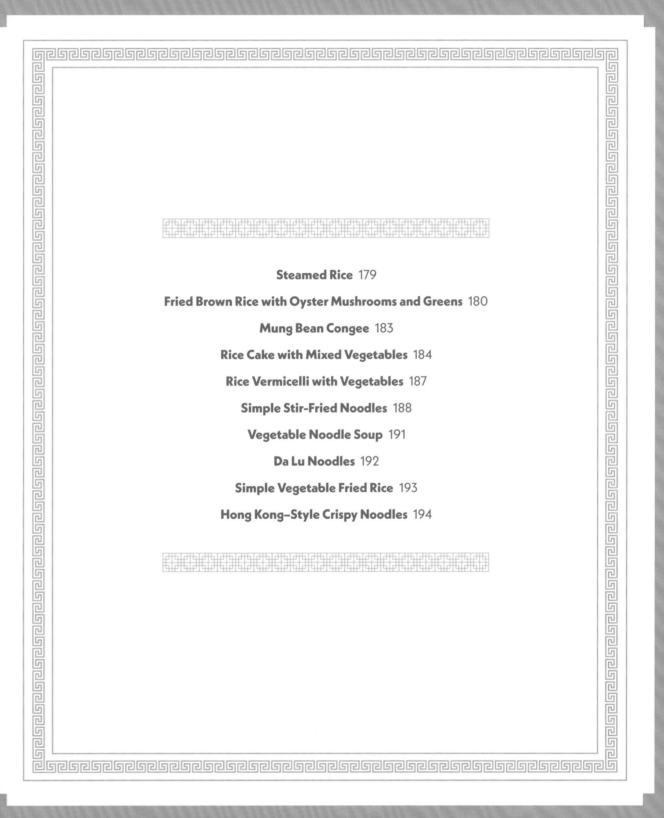

Steamed Rice 179

Fried Brown Rice with Oyster Mushrooms and Greens 180

Mung Bean Congee 183

Rice Cake with Mixed Vegetables 184

Rice Vermicelli with Vegetables 187

Simple Stir-Fried Noodles 188

Vegetable Noodle Soup 191

Da Lu Noodles 192

Simple Vegetable Fried Rice 193

Hong Kong–Style Crispy Noodles 194

There is so much art in how rice and noodles are produced, cooked, eaten, and revered. Both are staples across Chinese regional cuisines. In northern China where wheat is grown, noodles and other wheat-based products are predominant. In the southern half of China, where rice grows, rice and rice-based products are common. That's not to say that either region exclusively eats one or the other type of starch. But the culture has evolved from those respective agrarian points of view.

How profoundly does rice influence Chinese culture? When we greet one another, it is customary to ask whether the other person has eaten yet: *"Nǐ chī fàn le ma?"* The literal translation of the greeting is "Have you eaten rice yet?" The word *fàn* is "rice" and the term also represents "meal" as in, "Have you had a meal? Have you had rice?" Ironically, you could ask someone if they've had a meal/rice and then proceed to eat a bowl of noodle soup.

One of the cultural divides that I witness frequently is the habit that many have of dousing plain rice or noodles with soy sauce. This is not the Chinese way. A bowl of freshly steamed rice or boiled noodles is not a canvas for an indiscriminate amount of soy sauce. Rice should be appreciated for its aroma, and the dishes that you eat with it enhance the rice. Noodles should have a soft-yet-springy texture that's complemented by savory vegetables and/or pickles. Shifting perspective to hold rice and noodles in esteem is not a value that I think will resonate with the soy sauce offenders. But one can hope.

As you embark on this chapter, slow down for a moment to consider the flavors of the rice and noodles themselves. The aroma of rice is meant to be experienced and appreciated. If the rice isn't aromatic, perhaps it's time to try a different type of rice. Noodles are about texture and whether they have that spring when you bite into them. Soggy, overcooked noodles won't cut it. Take a moment, and then consider how other ingredients are the supporting actors that orbit the main characters and convey a complete landscape of tastes.

蒸飯

Steamed Rice

MAKES 4 CUPS RICE

2 cups medium- or long-grain white rice or brown rice

2½ cups water

If you have a rice cooker, cook your rice according to your preferences. If you don't have a rice cooker, you can make rice on the stove. Here are basic instructions for white and brown rice. Brown rice takes longer to cook, so plan accordingly.

■ Put the rice in a large fine-mesh sieve or a colander with small holes. Rinse the rice for about 1 minute under running water. Alternatively, you can put the rice in a large bowl, cover with water, run your hand through the rice a few times, pour out the water without spilling the rice, and repeat the process several times.

■ Put the rice in a 2-quart pot with a heavy bottom. Add the water and cover the pot with a lid. (If you plan ahead, you can let the rice soak for 30 minutes to help the heat penetrate the grains more easily.) Bring to a boil over high heat, which should take about 3 minutes. Don't walk away during this time. Reduce the heat to low. Cock the lid slightly to let the steam escape as you cook. For white rice, cook for 25 to 30 minutes, or until all the water has been absorbed and the rice is no longer soggy. For brown rice, cook for 30 to 35 minutes. Remove the pot from the heat and let the rice rest in the pot, covered, for 10 to 15 minutes to let the rice finish steaming.

IS A FANCY RICE COOKER WORTH IT?

For me, yes. If you eat a lot of rice, it's definitely worth buying a cooker. I think the only time my family didn't use a rice cooker was just after we immigrated to the United States when we barely had any housewares at all. A basic, one-button rice cooker can carry you far. But if you're willing to spend more money, you can dive into the latest induction rice cookers that offer specific settings to match different types of rice and texture preferences. For a long time, I couldn't bring myself to spend more than seventy-five dollars on a rice cooker. I wanted something one step better than the basic but couldn't imagine spending three hundred dollars or more

on a high-end induction rice cooker. My gearhead husband has no compunctions, however, about buying such a machine. He's the reason we have a top-of-the-line Zojirushi induction rice cooker. It cooks every type of rice, with dedicated settings that include soaking time—which is why the overall cooking time is longer. And, I have to admit, I was ecstatic when the package arrived. The rice cooks evenly every time, and the whoosh of aroma that wafts out when I first pop open the lid after the cooker alerts us it's done is one of my favorite moments. When the nuanced flavor of rice is so intrinsic to your culture, how you prepare rice is never an afterthought.

糙米炒飯＋杏鮑菇配蔬菜

Fried Brown Rice

with Oyster Mushrooms and Greens

**MAKES 4 SERVINGS AS A SIDE DISH
OR 2 SERVINGS AS A MEAL**

5 cups cold cooked brown rice

1½ tablespoons vegetable oil, divided

2 eggs, beaten

2 stalks green onions, finely chopped

⅔ cup oyster mushrooms, larger
pieces halved

1 cup sliced yu choy or *gai lan* (½-inch
pieces)

1½ tablespoons soy sauce

1 teaspoon black bean garlic sauce

⅛ teaspoon white pepper powder

Kosher salt (optional)

Suggested pairings: Sweet Potatoes
with Shallot-Chili Sauce (page 174) or
your choice of dishes

The nuttiness of brown rice is heightened in fried rice. Oyster mushrooms
are hearty and complement the greens. This can be the main dish or it can
play a supporting role. If you have leftovers, you can combine it with some
vegetable broth and you'll get a great soup.

■   Fluff the rice by breaking up any big clumps with a rice paddle or a fork.

■   Preheat a wok over medium-low heat until wisps of smoke rise from the
surface. Add ½ tablespoon of the oil and heat until it starts to shimmer. Add
the egg and scramble to cook until just done. Turn off the heat. The curds
should not be hard cooked. Transfer the egg to a dish and set aside. Clean out
the wok, scraping out any remnants of egg and rinsing with water, if needed.

■   Return the wok to the stove over high heat. Add the remaining 1 tablespoon oil. Add the onions and stir-fry for about 5 seconds. Add the mushrooms
and stir-fry for 30 seconds. Add the greens and stir-fry another 30 seconds.
Stir in the egg. Turn the heat to medium low. Add the rice and stir to combine.
Using the edge of the wok spatula blade, make gentle chopping motions to
break up any remaining clumps. Continue to stir and toss the rice to distribute
the heat. Add the soy sauce and black bean garlic sauce, and stir to combine.
Once incorporated, turn the heat to medium high to give the rice a bit of sear
for a few seconds. Add the white pepper powder. Toss again and let sear a
few seconds. Turn off the heat. Taste the rice for seasoning and adjust with
salt as needed. Stir again.

綠豆稀飯
Mung Bean Congee

MAKES 2 TO 4 SERVINGS

4 cups water, plus more as needed

½ cup medium- or long-grain uncooked rice

½ cup mung beans, soaked in 1½ cups water overnight

Condiments as desired, such as pickled radish, century egg, fermented chili tofu, minced ginger, chopped green onions, or soy sauce

Suggested pairing: Hot-and-Sour Celery, Carrots, and Bean Sprouts (page 150)

Congee is soothing and can be eaten any time of day, though it's usually a breakfast food. Congee is my oatmeal. As a child, I preferred eating it with just a dash of sugar. As my palate evolved, I graduated to having congee with savory condiments. This version with mung beans is my mother's favorite. She usually eats a bowl with nothing more than the congee itself.

■ Bring the water to a boil in a medium pot. Add the rice and beans, and stir. Turn the heat to low and simmer for 30 minutes. At about 30 minutes, the rice and beans should be tender and the consistency should be thick. Some people prefer the rice to be broken down even more. If so, add another 2 cups water, stir, and continue to simmer for 10 to 20 minutes. The longer the rice simmers, the more broken down and thicker it will become. You can add a touch more water if you prefer the congee to be looser.

素菜炒年糕

Rice Cake

with Mixed Vegetables

MAKES 4 SERVINGS

2 cups sliced rice cake

3 cups hot tap water or water that's been microwaved for 30 seconds

1 tablespoon vegetable oil

2 cups leafy greens, such as baby bok choy, yu choy (cut into ½-inch pieces), or baby spinach leaves

4 medium dried shiitake mushrooms, soaked in hot water for 30 minutes to reconstitute and cut into ¼-inch-thick pieces

½ cup sliced carrots (⅛ inch thick)

½ cup bean sprouts

1½ tablespoons soy sauce

1 tablespoon black bean garlic sauce

¼ teaspoon sesame oil

Suggested pairings: Ginger-Scallion Pea Shoots (page 137) or Garlic Yam Leaf (page 131)

Rice cakes are available sliced, marble-shaped, and in batons. Look for them in the refrigerated aisle of Asian grocery stores. There are dried versions, but the refrigerated version is widely available and easier to work with. I like the slices because there's more surface area for the sauce. You can use any combination of vegetables and seasonings, so feel free to experiment with flavors. Rice cake is also served at Lunar New Year because the Mandarin name *nian gao* ("sticky cake") is a homophone for the *nian*, which means "year," and *gao*, which means "tall" or "high." When you stick those years together, you're wishing others longevity.

■ In a medium bowl, soak the rice cake in the hot water for 2 to 3 minutes, then drain all but about ½ cup water. Set aside.

■ Preheat a wok over high heat until wisps of smoke rise from the surface. Swirl in the vegetable oil and let heat for a few seconds until it starts to shimmer. Add the greens and stir-fry for about 15 seconds. Add the mushrooms, carrots, and bean sprouts. Stir to combine. Add the rice cake and the reserved water, soy sauce, and black bean garlic sauce. Stir-fry for 2 minutes, or until well combined and the rice cake slices have softened. Finish with the sesame oil. Serve while hot.

素菜炒米粉

Rice Vermicelli

with Vegetables

MAKES 4 SERVINGS AS A SIDE DISH OR 2 SERVINGS AS A MEAL

1 tablespoon vegetable oil

2 stalks green onions, finely chopped

½ medium carrot, julienned (about ½ cup)

1 stalk celery, sliced ⅛ inch thick on the bias

2 cups baby spinach leaves

1 cup beech mushrooms, separated

⅓ pound dried vermicelli noodles (also called rice stick), soaked in warm water for 20 minutes to soften

2 tablespoons soy sauce

2 tablespoons water

1 tablespoon hoisin sauce

½ teaspoon sesame oil

Suggested pairings: Dry-Fried Brussels Sprouts (page 144) or Chinese Mustard Greens with Shishito Peppers (page 147)

Back in my family's restaurant days in the 1980s and '90s, there were many dishes that didn't sell because they were unfamiliar. Dry-fried green beans, stir-fried potato strips, hot-and-sour cabbage, and rice vermicelli were among them. When customer demand forced us to shift to buffet-style, we included all of these dishes and many others. That's when people learned to love rice vermicelli. I always keep a pack in the pantry and can make these noodles in a flash, using whatever veggies and protein I have on hand. This recipe will get you started.

■ Preheat a wok over high heat until wisps of smoke rise from the surface. Swirl in the vegetable oil and let heat for a few seconds until it starts to shimmer. Add the onions and stir-fry for about 10 seconds. Add the carrot and celery, and stir for about 30 seconds. Add the spinach and mushrooms and stir. Turn the heat down to medium. Add the noodles and stir-fry for 1 minute to combine. Add the soy sauce, water, hoisin sauce, and sesame oil. Stir-fry for 1 to 2 minutes, or until all the ingredients are incorporated. Serve while hot.

Simple Stir-Fried Noodles

MAKES 4 SERVINGS

¾ pound dried medium or wide Chinese noodles

1 teaspoon vegetable oil

1 stalk green onion, thinly sliced on the bias

½ medium carrot, julienned (about ½ cup)

8 snow peas, stemmed

2 cups roughly chopped greens, such as baby bok choy, Chinese cabbage, yu choy, or *gai lan* (Chinese broccoli)

½ water

2 tablespoons soy sauce

1 teaspoon minced fresh ginger

1 large clove garlic, crushed

½ teaspoon sesame oil

Suggested pairing: Spiced Tofu with Leeks and Cabbage (page 203)

When I walk down the dried or fresh noodle aisle at the Asian market, I see so many opportunities for discovery. Between a thin noodle and a wavy, wide hand-shaved noodle is a lot of territory. This dish can be whatever you want it to be, which is to say that you can use any number of noodle types and any combination of vegetables. Keep the same proportions, but experiment with the ingredients.

▪ Bring a large pot of water to a boil over high heat. Add the noodles and cook for 9 to 11 minutes, or until the noodles are soft but not mushy. Keep an eye on the water so it doesn't boil over. One trick is to keep a cup of cold water on hand and splash a bit into the pot when it looks like it's bubbling too fast. The cooking time will depend on the thickness of the noodles. Have a colander ready in the sink. When done, drain the noodles and set aside.

▪ Preheat a wok over high heat until wisps of smoke rise from the surface. Add the vegetable oil and heat until it starts to shimmer. Add the onion and stir for 5 seconds to release the aroma. Add the carrots and snow peas. Stir for about 10 seconds, add the greens, and stir-fry for an additional 15 seconds or so. Add the noodles, water, soy sauce, ginger, and garlic. Stir-fry actively for 1 to 2 minutes, or until all the ingredients are incorporated. Drizzle with the sesame oil and stir again. Serve.

Vegetable Noodle Soup

MAKES 4 SERVINGS

¾ pound dried medium Chinese noodles

6 cups Vegetable Broth (page 109)

1 teaspoon kosher salt

¼ teaspoon sesame oil

⅛ teaspoon white pepper powder

1 tablespoon vegetable oil

2 stalks green onions, finely chopped

½ cup roughly chopped fresh tomatoes

½ cup sliced shiitake mushrooms (use the mushrooms that flavored the broth)

2 cups julienned Persian or English cucumber (if using an English cucumber, peel it first)

1½ tablespoons soy sauce

1 tablespoon water

1 cup bean sprouts, divided

Suggested pairing: Chili Radish in Soy Sauce (page 243).

This is inspired by a Taiwanese noodle soup often sold on the streets. The original is flavored with shrimp and bits of ground pork. This version gets its hint of the sea from the kelp that's used to make the broth. The clear broth is meant to be light—even in the original—but you can take liberties and add hot sauce to taste.

■ Cook the noodles according to the package instructions. In the meantime, heat the vegetable broth with the salt in a medium pot and keep it at a low simmer. Add the sesame oil and white pepper powder. Stir to combine and keep warm.

■ Preheat a wok over high heat until wisps of smoke rise from the surface. Add the vegetable oil and heat until the surface starts to shimmer. Add the onions and stir for 5 seconds. Add the tomatoes and mushrooms and stir-fry for about 30 seconds. Add the cucumber, stir, and add the soy sauce and water. Stir-fry for 1 to 2 minutes, or until the tomatoes have cooked down. Turn off the heat.

■ Divide the noodles among four bowls. Top with broth. Divide the vegetables among the bowls. Garnish with the bean sprouts.

Da Lu Noodles

MAKES 4 SERVINGS

6 cups Vegetable Broth (page 109) or water

1 cup bamboo shoot strips

⅓ cup soy sauce

¼ cup dried wood ear mushrooms, soaked in warm water for 15 to 20 minutes

6 medium dried shiitake mushrooms, soaked in hot water for 30 minutes to reconstitute and sliced ¼-inch thick

¼ cup dried lily flowers, soaked in warm water for 15 minutes

Kosher salt

⅓ cup cornstarch mixed with ½ cup water

2 eggs, beaten

½ teaspoon sesame oil

¼ teaspoon white pepper powder

¾ pound dried medium Chinese noodles

Finely chopped green onions, for garnish (optional)

Fresh cilantro, for garnish (optional)

Suggested pairing: Yu Choy with Fried Shallots (page 132)

This is a humble Northern Chinese noodle dish that is made with everyday ingredients and has many interpretations. Versions range from noodles with gravy to noodles in a soup. I grew up with my mother's soup version. It was savory and always soothing. Back in our restaurant days, we always had large batches of hot-and-sour soup on the steam table, ready to portion out for customers who ordered it. To that soup, which had some similarities with this soup, I sometimes would add cooked noodles to make a "life hack" version of da lu *mian* (noodles).

▪ In a medium pot, combine the broth or water with the bamboo shoots, soy sauce, wood ear, shiitake, and lily flowers. Bring to a boil, then reduce the heat to medium low. Let simmer for about 5 minutes. Taste the broth. If it doesn't taste salty enough, add ¼ teaspoon kosher salt, or to taste. Slowly stir in the cornstarch slurry. Keep stirring until the slurry has been well combined and the broth thickens a bit. Drizzle on the eggs in thin ribbons. Stir immediately to break up the egg threads. Add the sesame oil and white pepper powder and stir well. Taste again for seasoning. If needed, add salt to taste. Reduce the heat to low and keep the soup warm while the noodles cook.

▪ Bring a separate big pot of water to a boil. Cook the noodles according to the package instructions. Drain the noodles and portion among four bowls. Ladle the soup over the noodles. Top with a sprinkle of green onions and cilantro.

素菜炒飯

Simple Vegetable Fried Rice

MAKES 4 SERVINGS AS A SIDE DISH OR 2 SERVINGS AS A MEAL

5 cups cold cooked rice

1½ tablespoons vegetable oil, divided

2 eggs, beaten

2 stalks green onions, finely chopped

1 cup sliced leafy greens (½-inch pieces), such as baby bok choy, Chinese cabbage, or yu choy

¼ cup carrots, sliced paper-thin

½ cup bean sprouts

2 tablespoons soy sauce

⅛ teaspoon white pepper powder

Kosher salt (optional)

Suggested pairings: Serve with your choice of dishes.

Cold rice is best for fried rice, so I always make extra rice to ensure there are leftovers. Before chilling, be sure to break up the rice a bit with a rice paddle or a fork. This will prevent the rice from becoming a brick. Fried rice can be plain (just egg) or it can contain any number of vegetables and seasonings. I love curry fried rice, so I will often add a teaspoon or so of curry powder to fried rice. If you prefer more pungency, you can add extra onions, garlic, hot sauce, and such.

■ Fluff the rice by breaking up any big clumps with a rice paddle or a fork.

■ Preheat a wok over medium-low heat until wisps of smoke rise from the surface. Add ½ tablespoon of the oil, and heat until it starts to shimmer. Add the eggs and scramble to cook until just done. Turn off the heat. The curds should not be hard cooked. Transfer the eggs to a dish and set aside. Clean out the wok, scraping out any remnants of egg and rinsing with water, if needed.

■ Return the wok to the stove over high heat. Add the remaining 1 table-spoon oil. Add the onions and stir-fry for about 5 seconds. Add the greens and carrots, and stir-fry for 1 minute, or until the greens have softened a bit. Stir in the eggs and bean sprouts. Turn the heat to medium low. Add the rice and stir to combine. Using the edge of the wok spatula blade, make gentle chopping motions to break up any remaining clumps. Continue to stir and toss the rice to distribute the heat. Add the soy sauce and stir to combine. Once incorporated, turn the heat to medium high to give the rice a bit of sear for a few seconds. Add the white pepper powder. Toss again and let sear a few seconds. Turn off the heat. Taste the rice for seasoning. If needed, add salt to taste. Stir again and serve.

Hong Kong–Style Crispy Noodles

MAKES 4 SERVINGS

For the noodles:

6 cups water

8 to 10 ounces fresh Chinese noodles

Vegetable oil, for frying

For the topping:

2 teaspoons vegetable oil

2 stalks green onions, cut into 2-inch segments

1 cup julienned carrots

4 to 6 medium dried shiitake mushrooms, soaked in hot water for 2 to 3 hours, stemmed, and cut into ¼-inch-thick pieces

1 cup roughly chopped *gai lan* (Chinese broccoli) or other leafy green

8 snow peas, stemmed

1 cup bean sprouts

1 tablespoon soy sauce

1 tablespoon black bean garlic sauce

⅔ cup water

1 teaspoon cornstarch mixed with 2 teaspoons water

¼ teaspoon sesame oil

⅛ teaspoon white pepper powder

Suggested pairings: Kung Pao Tofu Puffs (page 199) or Zucchini Egg Crepe (page 232)

My father loved this dish. When we traveled and ate at Chinese restaurants, he would look for this dish and order it. The Mandarin name translates roughly to "double-sided golden-brown." Cooked noodles are then fried in the shape of a cake, which then serves as a canvas for mixed stir-fried vegetables and protein in a gravy-like sauce. The intersection of textures and flavors—crunchy-chewy noodles, crisp-yet-tender vegetables, savory sauce—is a joy to eat.

■ To make the noodles, bring the water to a boil in a medium pot. Cook the noodles for about 2 minutes. Drain well and set aside. Add about ⅛ inch of vegetable oil to a heavy 8- or 9-inch skillet, such as a cast iron. Heat the oil over medium heat until the surface starts to shimmer. Test the temperature by placing a small strand of noodle in the oil. If it immediately fries, the oil is ready. Place half of the noodles in the pan, making sure to arrange the noodles in a disc. Fry on each side for 2 to 3 minutes, or until golden-to-dark brown but not burnt. Repeat with the remaining noodles. Place on a serving plate and set aside while you make the vegetables.

■ To make the topping, preheat a wok over high heat until wisps of smoke rise from the surface. Add the vegetable oil and heat until the surface starts to shimmer. Add the onions and stir for 5 seconds. Add the carrots and mushrooms and stir for 10 seconds. Add the *gai lan* and stir for 30 seconds. Add the snow peas, bean sprouts, soy sauce, black bean garlic sauce, and water. Stir-fry for 1 to 2 minutes. Stir in the cornstarch slurry, making sure it gets well mixed with the sauce and vegetables. Finish with sesame oil and white pepper powder. Give it one last stir, then pour it over the noodles. Serve while hot.

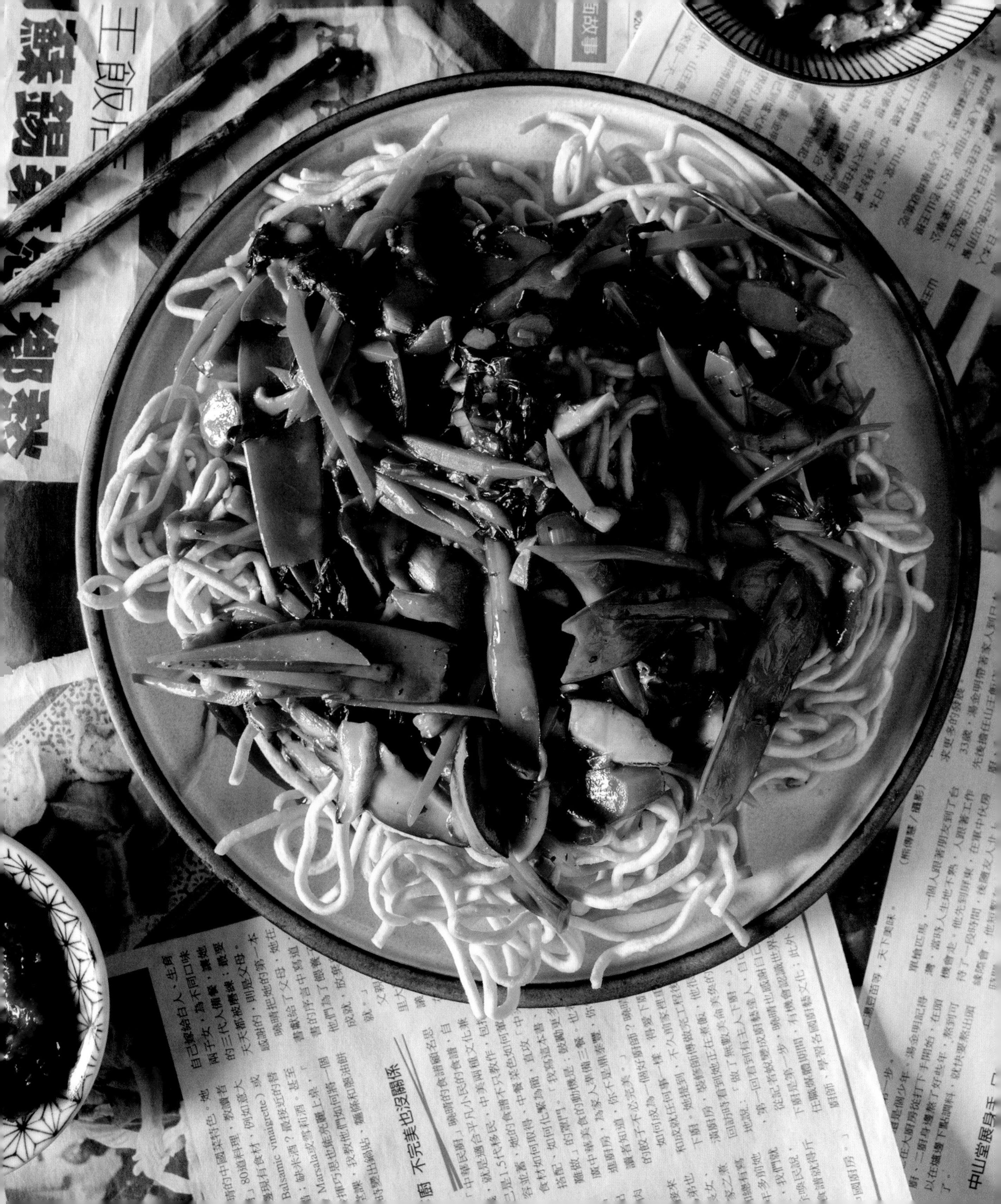

豆腐

Tofu

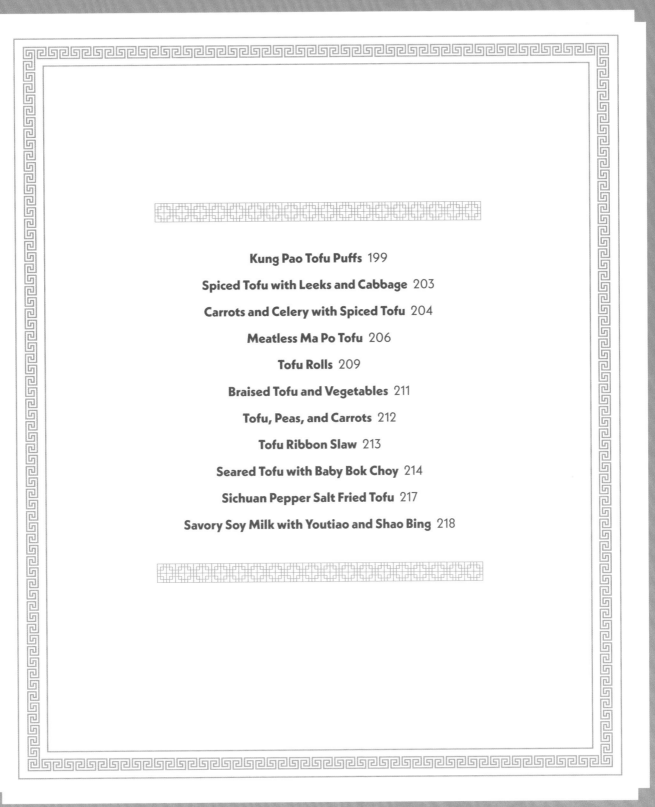

Kung Pao Tofu Puffs 199

Spiced Tofu with Leeks and Cabbage 203

Carrots and Celery with Spiced Tofu 204

Meatless Ma Po Tofu 206

Tofu Rolls 209

Braised Tofu and Vegetables 211

Tofu, Peas, and Carrots 212

Tofu Ribbon Slaw 213

Seared Tofu with Baby Bok Choy 214

Sichuan Pepper Salt Fried Tofu 217

Savory Soy Milk with Youtiao and Shao Bing 218

Tofu is such a chameleon. It can shapeshift from bean to milk to sheets, curds, pressed blocks, spiced squares, fried puffs, and fermented cubes. Across cultures and cuisines in Asia, tofu ingenuity is mind-boggling. How our ancestors discovered the potential of the soybean thousands of years ago is steeped in legends, but the first record of tofu comes from imperial China during the Han Dynasty (202 BC–220 AD). So the culture around tofu has a long history that cannot be hemmed in by the rise of health foods and diet trends.

For many of us, tofu (and soy milk) is a part of life. From our first bites as babies to our most recent meal, tofu has been a constant companion. We've never questioned its existence. So it's always jarring to read tofu described as bland or flavorless in contemporary food magazines and recipe websites. It's not flavorless. It has a distinct taste of soy milk. What registers as bland or flavorless to some is an essential flavor in dishes across the spectrum of savory, funky, spicy, smoky, sour, sweet, and delicate. The intention isn't to mask the flavor of tofu but to enhance it. In this aspect, tofu suffers a similar fate as steamed rice, which too often is treated as a vehicle for soy sauce.

But, if you're here, it likely means you're familiar with tofu and that you probably enjoy eating it. If you are fortunate enough to live in a city where there is a local tofu maker, be sure to explore buying directly or through their distributors. Tofu is best when freshly made. While making tofu yourself is straightforward, I don't cover that process in these pages. Quality tofu is so widely available and there are so many options for brands and texture types that making your own is not something I feel is necessary to emphasize.

An important reminder, though, is that tofu comes in many forms and styles and can vary by cuisine and the producer. Japanese silken tofu is delicate and not ideal for the tumble of stir-fries. Chinese soft tofu, likewise, is tender and best suited for gentle cooking methods. Chinese medium and firm tofu can withstand active stir-frying. Other tofu products, such as tofu puffs and spiced tofu, are versatile and can hold up in any number of preparations. Texture as much as taste can affect whether you prefer one over another type of tofu, so you may have to do some experimenting.

宫保油豆腐

Kung Pao Tofu Puffs

MAKES 4 SERVINGS

For the sauce:

2 tablespoons water

1 tablespoon soy sauce

1½ teaspoons bean sauce

1 teaspoon minced fresh ginger

2 teaspoons chili sauce

2 large cloves garlic, minced

½ teaspoon ground Sichuan peppercorns (optional)

For the tofu mixture:

1 tablespoon vegetable oil

1 cup diced sweet bell peppers (about 1-inch dice)

2 stalks green onions, finely chopped

1 package tofu puffs (about 6 ounces) or 1 batch Tofu Puffs (recipe follows)

¼ cup Huang Fei Hong Hot Chilli Pepper Peanuts or roasted unsalted peanuts

Suggested pairings: Simply Steamed Baby Bok Choy (page 160) or Gai Lan with Oyster Mushrooms (page 148)

Tofu puffs are fried cubes of soft tofu that, when cooled, become slightly chewy and spongy. The texture holds up well in this kung pao preparation. You can buy tofu puffs in packages at an Asian market. They can be labeled bean curd puffs, soy puffs, tofu pouches, tofu beignets, tofu soufflé—and likely other terms that are country specific. While making your own tofu puffs (recipe follows) is an extra step, the freshness can make a difference in the final dish.

▪ To make the sauce, in a small bowl, combine the water, soy sauce, bean sauce, ginger, chili sauce, garlic, and Sichuan peppercorns. Set aside.

▪ To make the tofu mixture, preheat a wok over high heat until wisps of smoke rise from the surface. Add the oil and heat until it starts to shimmer. Add the bell peppers, and stir for about 1 minute. Add the onions, tofu, and peanuts, and stir for a few seconds to combine. Add the sauce, and stir-fry thoroughly to distribute. Stir-fry for about 2 minutes to let the sauce meld with the tofu puffs. Serve with rice.

→

Tofu Puffs

MAKES 16 PIECES

1 quart vegetable oil

1 (16-ounce) package soft tofu (not silken)

While I prefer soft tofu for this preparation, you can use medium-firm or firm tofu. Because the shape of tofu can vary, use your best judgment when cutting a block into cubes.

■ In a 2-quart pot or Dutch oven, heat the oil to 375 degrees F.

■ Meanwhile, prepare the tofu. Line a plate or small tray with a double layer of paper towels. Remove the tofu from the package, draining the liquid into the sink. Place the tofu on the paper towels. Using another sheet of paper towel, gently dab the surface of the tofu to absorb some of the residual liquid. Place the tofu on a cutting board, with the long edge facing you.

■ Cut the tofu in half crosswise as if you were creating a layer cake. Next, imagine there's an outline of an ice cube tray on the tofu and make one cut down the center of the tofu lengthwise. Then, make four cuts crosswise. You will end up with 16 pieces of tofu.

■ Using a candy thermometer, check the temperature of the oil. When it has reached 375 degrees F, you are ready to fry. Line a plate with paper towels. Using a heatproof slotted spoon or skimmer, gently place as many pieces of tofu as will fit in your pot without crowding. The tofu pieces will need room to float. Let fry until golden brown on all sides, 2 to 3 minutes. Remove from the oil and place on a paper towel–lined plate to drain. Repeat the process with the remaining tofu cubes. Use right away, or let cool to room temperature and store in an airtight container in the refrigerator for up to 3 days.

蒜苗白菜炒豆乾

Spiced Tofu

with Leeks and Cabbage

MAKES 4 SERVINGS

5 to 6 ounces spiced tofu (about 2 thick 2½-inch squares)

2 cups Taiwanese cabbage or regular green cabbage, cut into 1-inch squares

¼ teaspoon kosher salt

1 tablespoon vegetable oil

1 dried red chili pepper, halved, or ½ teaspoon dried red pepper flakes

1 cup sliced leeks, white part only, ⅛ inch thick

1 tablespoon soy sauce

1 tablespoon water

1½ teaspoons black bean garlic sauce

Suggested pairings: Yu Choy with Fried Shallots (page 132) or Savory Mushrooms with Rice Powder (page 159)

I like this combination of ingredients because the spiced tofu, leeks, and cabbage can all handle a little bit of char from the wok. The textures and flavors are harmonious together and as an accompaniment to a steaming bowl of rice. Spiced tofu comes in different sizes, but you usually can find it in packs in Asian markets and some supermarkets. Depending on the size of the individual squares, you may need to adjust the amount you use. A little more or a little less won't affect the outcome of the dish.

■ Cut the tofu on the bias by holding your knife at a 45-degree angle, with the blade facing away from you. Slice the tofu about ¼ inch thick. Each piece should be roughly 1¼ inches by 2½ inches. This creates more surface area. In a large bowl, combine the cabbage with the salt. Work the salt into the cabbage leaves by gently squeezing handfuls of cabbage repeatedly for about 1 minute. Set aside.

■ Preheat a wok over high heat until wisps of smoke rise from the surface. Add the oil and heat until it starts to shimmer. Add the chili pepper and stir for several seconds. Add the leeks and stir-fry for about 15 seconds. Add the tofu and let the pieces sear for about 5 seconds. Add the cabbage and stir-fry for 30 to 60 seconds to soften. Add the soy sauce, water, and black bean garlic sauce. Stir-fry for 1 to 2 minutes until everything is well combined. Serve while hot.

豆乾炒胡蘿蔔芹菜絲

Carrots and Celery
with Spiced Tofu

MAKES 4 SERVINGS

1 tablespoon vegetable oil

5 to 6 ounces spiced tofu (about 2 thick 2½-inch squares), julienned

1 small whole jalapeño pepper, thinly sliced on the bias (optional)

1 cup julienned carrots

1 stalk celery, trimmed and sliced thinly on the bias

1 tablespoon soy sauce

1 tablespoon water

⅛ teaspoon salt or to taste (optional)

⅛ teaspoon sesame oil

Suggested pairings: Mung Bean Congee (page 183) or Fried Brown Rice with Oyster Mushrooms and Greens (page 180)

I didn't grow up eating raw carrot and celery sticks. I never understood it. But stir-fried celery and carrots is something else. It's important to slice the celery thinly and on the bias so that it can mingle better with the sauce. The addition of spiced tofu is a classic combination. Even when I was a child and didn't particularly like eating celery, I still appreciated its role in this dish. For those who eat meat, you can easily add bits of beef, pork, or chicken.

■ Preheat a wok over high heat until wisps of smoke rise from the surface. Add the vegetable oil and heat until it starts to shimmer. Add the tofu, spread it out across the bottom of the wok, and let sear for 5 to 10 seconds. Stir, then add the jalapeño, carrots, and celery. Stir-fry for 1 to 2 minutes to soften the vegetables. Add the soy sauce and water. Stir-fry for about 30 seconds. Taste for seasoning and add salt, if needed. Finish with the sesame oil.

素麻婆豆腐

Meatless Ma Po Tofu

MAKES 4 SERVINGS

1 (16-ounce) package medium-firm or soft (not silken) tofu, cut into cubes about 1 inch by ½ inch

2 cups water

1 teaspoon kosher salt, plus more to taste

2 tablespoons vegetable oil

2 stalks green onions, finely chopped

2 teaspoons minced fresh ginger

1 to 2 cloves garlic, minced or pushed through a garlic press

1 to 2 tablespoons chili bean sauce, or more to taste

2 tablespoons cornstarch mixed with 3 tablespoons water to create a slurry

1 teaspoon ground Sichuan peppercorns

¼ teaspoon sesame oil

1 to 2 tablespoons Chili Oil (recipe follows)

Suggested pairings: Dry-Fried Brussels Sprouts (page 144) and Eggplant with Black Bean Garlic Sauce (page 170)

The traditional version of this classic Sichuan dish includes a small amount of ground pork or beef and is topped with a generous amount of chili oil. I prefer to tone down the oil so that it doesn't obliterate my palate. It's important that the Sichuan peppercorns be fresh and lightly toasted in a dry pan over low heat before grinding The addition of the Sichuan peppercorns is what makes the dish. There are no substitutes and, if you skip it, then the tofu will be missing its signature numbing effect. If you can get Sichuan peppercorns from the Hanyuan region (TheMalaMarket.com is a good resource, though it frequently sells out), it will be quite the taste sensation.

- Place the tofu in a small pot and cover with the water and the 1 teaspoon salt. Bring to a simmer and then turn off the heat. Let the tofu steep in the hot water while you finish preparing the other ingredients.

- Heat a wok over high heat. Add the oil and heat for about 10 seconds. Add the onions, ginger, and garlic. Stir-fry quickly to keep them from burning.

- Add the chili bean sauce. Stir-fry well to combine. Gently add the tofu, with the steeping water. Very carefully stir the sauce and tofu to combine. Let simmer for 2 to 3 minutes.

- Add salt to taste. Gently stir in the cornstarch slurry to thicken the sauce. If it looks like it's getting too thick, then don't use all the slurry. Add the Sichuan peppercorns and give it one last gentle stir. Drizzle on the sesame oil. Before serving, add the chili oil on top of the tofu.

Chili Oil

MAKES ABOUT ⅓ CUP OIL

½ cup vegetable oil

2 teaspoons toasted and ground Sichuan peppercorns

1½ tablespoons Chinese- or Korean-style chili powder

You can double or triple this recipe to make a larger quantity. Store in a glass canning jar for up to several months.

■ In a small pan over low heat, combine the oil, Sichuan peppercorns, and chili powder. Cook for 5 minutes, or until the oil starts to look red from the chili. Remove the pan from the heat, then pour the oil into a small heatproof bowl. Let it cool to room temperature.

豆腐捲

Tofu Rolls

MAKES 8 TO 10 ROLLS

For the filling:

1½ teaspoons vegetable oil

2 stalks green onions, finely chopped

2 cups sliced Chinese cabbage, about ¼ inch thick

1 cup bean sprouts

4 medium dried shiitake mushrooms, soaked in hot water for 30 minutes, stemmed, and cut ¼ inch thick

½ cup julienned carrots

1½ tablespoons soy sauce

¼ teaspoon sesame oil

¼ teaspoon kosher salt, or to taste

For the rolls:

1 (8-ounce) package tofu skin or spring roll soybean skin, or Havista fresh frozen soy skin

Vegetable oil, for frying

Suggested pairing: Hot-and-Sour Soup with Dried Lily Flowers (page 114)

Alternately called bean curd skin, spring roll soybean skin, and yuba, these skins are derived from the film that forms on the surface of simmering soy milk. You can buy these in large sheets, scraggly rolled logs, and a number of other shapes designed to be elegant enough to be packaged as gifts. The dried tofu skins are often broken up to include in soups and braises. For these fried spring rolls, you'll need the tofu skins that come in large sheets and resemble tan fruit leather. They're partially dried and are sold in the refrigerated section. Another option, if you can find it in your Asian market, is the "fresh frozen soy skin" from the Havista brand. These skins are about 8 by 8 inches in size and are perfect for making these rolls. They also stick to themselves, so no hydration is needed to seal.

■ To make the filling, preheat a wok over high heat until wisps of smoke rise from the surface. Add the vegetable oil and heat for a few seconds until the surface starts to shimmer. Add the onions and stir-fry for 10 seconds. Add the cabbage and stir-fry for 30 seconds. Add the bean sprouts, mushrooms, and carrots, and stir to combine. Add the soy sauce and stir-fry for 1 to 2 minutes, or until the cabbage has cooked down a bit. Finish with the sesame oil. Taste for seasoning and add the salt. Give it one last toss and transfer to a dish to cool.

■ To make the rolls, you can skip this next step if using the fresh frozen soy skin. For the other type of skin that requires soaking, unfold the tofu skin. With scissors, cut 10 squares that are 6 by 6 inches. Place one square into an 8-by-8-inch baking dish filled halfway with warm water. It will take 10 to 20 seconds for the skin to soften. Don't oversoak or it won't hold up. Carefully pick up the square and let any residual water drip off.

- Position the tofu wrapper with a corner pointing toward you. Place about ¼ cup filling in the center of the wrapper. Fold the bottom corner over the filling and carefully drag it back toward you with the filling firmly inside your grip. The idea is to begin to shape the roll and to get rid of any air pockets. Now, roll forward about halfway and fold the right flap over, followed by the left flap. Finish rolling and gently press the remaining corner to seal. Some recipes call for a flour paste to seal these, but I've found that if you soak the skin briefly, it will stick to itself. Set the finished roll on a plate or a small baking sheet. Repeat with the remaining rolls.

- If you have a deep fryer, set it up and heat oil to 350 degrees F. Otherwise, use a heavy-bottomed deep-sided skillet. Pour in oil about ½ inch deep. Heat over medium heat until the oil is 350 degrees F. Meanwhile, line a serving dish with a couple sheets of paper towel and set aside. In batches, place each roll flap side down in the oil. Be careful while frying, because the oil may pop. Fry 1 minute on each side, or until sandy brown. Place on the platter to drain any extra oil. Repeat with the remaining rolls. Serve with soy sauce on the side or your favorite sweet chili sauce.

豆腐煲

Braised Tofu and Vegetables

MAKES 4 SERVINGS

4 cups water

4 cups sliced Chinese cabbage (½-inch pieces)

6 medium dried shiitake mushrooms, soaked in hot water for 30 minutes, stemmed, and halved

About 7 ounces firm tofu, cut into ½-inch cubes

½ cup sliced carrots, ¼ inch thick

1 tablespoon soy sauce

8 snow peas, stemmed

¼ teaspoon kosher salt, or to taste

2 teaspoons cornstarch mixed with 1 tablespoon water to make a slurry

¼ teaspoon sesame oil

⅛ teaspoon white pepper powder

Chopped fresh cilantro, for garnish (optional)

Suggested pairing: Eggplant with Black Bean Garlic Sauce (page 170)

This is a dish that traditionally might be braised in a Chinese clay pot, or sand pot, which has a distinct sandy exterior and a glazed interior. The pots sit in a removable wire basket that helps protect it and transfer heat. Sand pot was one of my father's favorite dishes to order when we ate at Chinese restaurants in any big city we visited. Whatever delicacies were contained in the steaming, bubbling vessel, we always knew not to touch the pot itself or risk a serious burn. You can use a Dutch oven or similar heavy-bottomed pot.

■ In a medium pot, combine the water, cabbage, and mushrooms. Bring to a boil, then reduce the heat to medium low and let simmer for 10 to 15 minutes, or until the cabbage stems start to look translucent. Add the tofu, carrots, and soy sauce. Let simmer for about 5 minutes. Add the snow peas and stir. Taste the liquid for seasoning and add the salt. With a small rubber spatula or a spoon, carefully stir the ingredients as you swirl in the cornstarch slurry. This will help thicken the braising liquid. Be sure to stir carefully until the slurry has been well incorporated. Finish with the oil and white pepper powder. Serve topped with cilantro.

Tofu, Peas, and Carrots

MAKES 4 SERVINGS

1 teaspoon vegetable oil

1 stalk green onion, finely chopped

½ teaspoon minced fresh ginger

1 clove garlic, minced

2 cups water

¾ teaspoon salt, plus more as needed

About 7 ounces firm tofu, cut into ½-inch cubes

⅓ cup frozen peas and carrots

2 teaspoons cornstarch mixed with 1 tablespoon water to make a slurry

Kosher salt (optional)

¼ teaspoon sesame oil

⅛ teaspoon white pepper powder

Suggested pairings: Yu Choy with Fried Shallots (page 132) and Eggplant with Black Bean Garlic Sauce (page 170)

The simplicity of this dish is the appeal. It doesn't demand much cooking time, and it's easy to eat with a bowl of rice. It reminds me of *risi e bisi*, the Italian rice-and-peas dish that's made with fresh spring peas and is family-friendly. If you can get fresh peas in season, that would be fantastic. Otherwise, throw this together with frozen peas. Alternatively, you could use frozen shelled edamame and/or corn. The sauce is meant to be light, so this would be an ideal complement to dishes that are richer.

■ Heat the vegetable oil in a medium pot over medium heat until the surface shimmers. Add the onion, ginger, and garlic. Stir and let cook for 15 seconds. Add the water, salt, tofu, and peas and carrots. Turn the heat to high and bring to a boil. As soon as it boils, reduce the heat to medium low and let the tofu simmer for about 5 minutes. Swirl in the cornstarch slurry, stirring gently to prevent clumps. Stir for about 15 seconds. Taste for seasoning, and add salt, if needed. Finish with the sesame oil and white pepper powder.

錦繡豆腐絲

Tofu Ribbon Slaw

MAKES 4 SERVINGS

2 sheets five-spice tofu sheets

1 rib celery

1 small carrot, julienned

¼ cup salted peanuts or cashews, roughly chopped

1½ tablespoons soy sauce

1 tablespoon unseasoned rice vinegar

1 teaspoon sesame oil

1 teaspoon chili bean sauce

1 teaspoon chili oil

1 cup chopped fresh cilantro

Suggested pairing: Gai Lan with Oyster Mushrooms (page 148)

I was looking for tofu skin when I found tofu sheets. What's the difference? Tofu skin, also called yuba, is the film that forms on top of warm soy milk. The skin can be removed and dried, and then can be reconstituted and added to soups and stir-fries. Tofu sheet is firm tofu that's pressed into ⅛-inch-thick squares. Sliced into thin ribbons, the tofu can be mixed into a cold salad or tossed in a stir-fry. As with all tofu products, it's cooked and ready to eat, so a slaw is quick to assemble. This would make a great appetizer.

■ Stack the tofu sheets and cut in half. Stack the halves and, starting on the short side, slice thinly into ¼-inch-thick ribbons. Place the ribbons in a large bowl. Slice the celery on the bias into ¼-inch-thick pieces. Allow the celery slices to shingle naturally. Then, slice the shingled celery pieces into fine strips, about ⅛ inch thick. Add the celery, carrot, and nuts to the tofu.

■ In a small bowl, combine the soy sauce, vinegar, sesame oil, chili bean sauce, and chili oil. Stir to combine. Add the mixture to the slaw and toss well to combine. Add the cilantro and mix again. You can serve right away, but if you have time to let the slaw marinate for at least 30 minutes, it'll taste even better.

Seared Tofu

with Baby Bok Choy

MAKES 4 SERVINGS

About 7 ounces medium or firm tofu (half a standard block), cut into ½-inch-thick slices, then each square cut in half diagonally to create triangles

2 tablespoons soy sauce, divided

⅓ cup cornstarch, for dredging

2 tablespoons plus 1 teaspoon vegetable oil

3 cups sliced baby bok choy, about ½ inch thick

½ cup brown beech mushrooms or enoki mushrooms

2 cloves garlic, finely chopped

½ cup water

¼ teaspoon sesame oil

Suggested pairings: Cucumber and Cloud Ear Mushrooms (page 248) or Asparagus with Shiitake and Oyster Mushrooms (page 163)

We used to have a dish on the menu at my family's restaurant that included paired triangles of flash-fried tofu with vegetables and slices of barbecued pork. For this interpretation, I didn't want to fry the tofu, but I still wanted to give it another layer of flavor. The tofu is marinated, coated with a dusting of starch, and then seared. While I use baby bok choy in this recipe, you can opt for your choice of greens, such as *gai lan*, yu choy, spinach, or Chinese cabbage.

■ Place the tofu in a shallow dish and drizzle 1 tablespoon of the soy sauce over the pieces. Carefully turn the tofu a few times to coat with the soy sauce. Put the cornstarch in another shallow dish or plate. Dredge the tofu with the cornstarch, making sure the tofu pieces are evenly coated. In a medium skillet, heat 2 tablespoons of the vegetable oil over medium-low heat for about 1 minute. Place the tofu in the skillet, placing as many as will fit in the pan without overcrowding. Sear 1 to 2 minutes on each side, or until richly browned. Place the tofu on a clean plate. Repeat with any remaining tofu. Set aside.

■ Preheat a wok over high heat until wisps of smoke rise from the surface. Add the remaining 1 teaspoon vegetable oil and heat until it starts to shimmer. Add the bok choy and stir for 30 seconds. Add the mushrooms and garlic. Stir for a few seconds to combine. Add the water and stir to combine. Add the tofu and the remaining 1 tablespoon soy sauce, stirring carefully to combine. Reduce the heat to medium low and let simmer for 1 to 2 minutes, or until the sauce is slightly thickened. Finish with sesame oil.

椒鹽豆腐

Sichuan Pepper Salt Fried Tofu

MAKES 4 APPETIZER SERVINGS

About 14 ounces tofu, cut into 1-inch cubes

¼ teaspoon kosher salt

Vegetable oil

1 cup cornstarch, for dredging

¾ teaspoon Sichuan Pepper Salt, or to taste (recipe follows)

Suggested pairing: Ma La Succotash (page 257)

Tofu isn't boring, but I acknowledge that there are plenty of people for whom tofu is an acquired taste. I think fried tofu with the numbing Sichuan peppercorns might offer enough punch to sway their minds. If you love tofu, you might consider doubling the recipe because it's hard to stop eating them. Fair warning: The fried tofu fresh out of hot oil can be hazardous to your tongue. Be very careful when you eat these because you naturally will want to pop them in your mouth like popcorn.

- Place the tofu cubes on a small baking tray and sprinkle with the salt.

- In a heavy-bottomed skillet, add oil to a ¼-inch depth. Heat over medium low for 1 to 2 minutes, or until the surface starts to shimmer. Line a plate with paper towels and set aside.

- Place a few pieces of the tofu at a time in the cornstarch and coat evenly. Fry the tofu in batches for about 1 minute on one side. Flip to the opposite side and fry for 1 minute, or until golden. When done, place on the lined plate to drain any excess oil. Repeat with the remaining tofu. Sprinkle with Sichuan Pepper Salt and serve while hot.

Sichuan Pepper Salt

MAKES ABOUT 3 TABLESPOONS PEPPER SALT

2 tablespoons whole Sichuan peppercorns

1 teaspoon white pepper powder

1 tablespoon sea salt or kosher salt

Sprinkle this on anything that might need a kick of numbing spices.

- Pick through the peppercorns and discard any large loose stems. Don't worry about the tiny ones.

- In a small skillet over medium heat, toast the peppercorns for 2 minutes, or until fragrant. Gently shake the pan as the peppercorns toast to keep them from burning. Remove from the heat and transfer to a plate to cool. Grind the peppercorns to a fine powder in a spice grinder. In a small bowl, combine the peppercorns, white pepper powder, and salt, and mix well. This can be stored in an airtight container on the counter for several months.

燒餅油條加豆漿

Savory Soy Milk
with Youtiao and Shao Bing

MAKES 1 SERVING

1 cup unsweetened soy milk

1 teaspoon finely chopped pickles, such as Chinese mustard greens, chili radish, cucumber, or preserved vegetable (these are all available in Asian markets)

1 to 2 teaspoons Chinese black vinegar or your favorite vinegar

1 teaspoon finely chopped green onion

¼ teaspoon sesame oil

⅛ teaspoon white pepper powder (optional)

1 *youtiao*, cut into 1-inch pieces (recipe follows)

Shao bing (recipe follows)

Leave it to the Chinese to turn a bowl of soy milk into an event. When you go to a *doujiang* shop, where they make fresh soy milk daily, they offer it to you savory or sweet, hot or cold. Then you can order an accompanying *shao bing* (sesame flatbread) or *youtiao* (Chinese doughnut), or "a set," which is a *shao bing youtiao* sandwich—a doughnut sandwich. You dip the sandwich into the soy milk. I'm taking the shortcut of using store-bought soy milk, but *youtiao* and *shao bing* are better fresh and are worth the extra effort. This will take planning ahead to time all the pieces: The *youtiao* dough needs to rest overnight. The *shao bing* can be made up to a day ahead and reheated in the oven or toaster.

▪ In a small pot over medium heat, heat the soy milk until it starts to bubble. Pour into a bowl and add the pickles, vinegar, onion, oil, white pepper powder, and *youtiao*. The vinegar causes the soy milk to curdle, which is intentional. Serve with *shao bing*. Eat while hot.

Youtiao

(Chinese "Doughnuts")

MAKES 8 TO 10 PIECES

2 cups all-purpose flour

2 teaspoons baking powder

½ teaspoon baking soda

½ teaspoon kosher salt

2 tablespoons vegetable oil, plus more for frying

¾ cup water

The dough must chill overnight and then have enough time to warm up before you cut and fry them, so this requires planning if you expect to have them fresh in the morning.

■ In a medium bowl, combine the flour, baking powder, baking soda, and salt. Add the 2 tablespoons oil and the water. Stir until clumps begin to form. Gather the dough together until you get a ball. Knead for 2 to 3 minutes to incorporate. Place the dough in the bowl and cover the bowl with plastic wrap. Let rest for about 30 minutes. Knead the dough again for 2 to 3 minutes, or until smooth. Press the dough into a 6-by-8-inch rectangular disc. Wrap with plastic wrap and chill in the refrigerator overnight. In the morning, take the dough out and set it on the counter to warm up for at least 1 hour, if possible.

■ If you have a deep fryer, set it up and heat oil to 350 degrees F. Otherwise, fill a large Dutch oven with oil about 4 inches deep. Heat to 350 degrees F. Meanwhile, roll out the dough in a rectangle that's about 20 by 5 inches. Cut the dough into 16 to 20 even strips. Take a pair of dough strips and stack them together. Repeat with the remaining strips, trying your best to match similar strips. You should have 8 to 10 pairs. Take a chopstick and place it lengthwise in the middle of the dough. Press down hard to create an indentation and to adhere the top piece of dough to the bottom piece. But don't press so hard that you cut through the dough. Repeat with the remaining pairs.

■ Line a baking sheet with paper towels. When the oil is ready, fry the dough in batches. Use your fingertips to pick up each end of one strip. Give it a gentle stretch as you carefully place it in the oil. It will fry, puff up, and turn a rich golden color within seconds. Turn a few times to ensure even frying. Remove from the oil and place on the baking sheet. Repeat with the remaining dough. Serve right away. Unlike Western-style doughnuts that are sweet, *youtiao* are eaten unadorned or are used as a filling or condiment. Leftovers can be wrapped and kept on the counter for up to 2 days. I flatten them and pop them in the toaster to crisp up. (For my kids, I did toss a couple of these in cinnamon sugar.)

Shao Bing

(Sesame Flatbread)

MAKES 8 FLATBREADS

For the roux:

¼ cup vegetable oil

¼ cup all-purpose flour

For the *shao bing*:

3 cups all-purpose flour, plus more for dusting

⅔ cup boiling water

⅓ cup cold tap water

1 to 2 tablespoons warm tap water, plus more for brushing the dough

1 teaspoon kosher salt

¼ cup sesame seeds

Shao bing, or sesame flatbread, can be made ahead and frozen. You can pop them in the toaster to heat. Or, if you plan ahead, you can make them fresh for breakfast.

■ To make the roux, in a small pan over medium heat, heat the oil for 1 minute, or until the surface starts to shimmer slightly. Add the flour and, using a heatproof spatula or a small whisk, stir quickly to combine. Reduce the heat to low. Stir the mixture constantly for about 3 minutes, or until the color of the roux resembles peanut butter. Remove the pan from the heat. Continue to stir for about 1 minute, letting the residual heat from the pan brown the roux even more. Scrape the roux into a heatproof bowl and set aside.

■ To make the *shao bing*, put the flour in a large bowl. Add the boiling water and, using a spatula or a wooden spoon, stir quickly to distribute. Add the cold water and stir to combine. As the dough forms, you can use your hands to start bringing the dough together. If it feels too dry, you can add 1 to 2 tablespoons warm tap water. Once you've worked all the flour into the mound of dough, take the dough out of the bowl and knead it on a work surface for 2 minutes, or until smooth. The dough should feel damp but not sticky.

■ Lightly dust your work surface with flour. Roll out the dough into a rectangle about 18 inches long by 12 inches wide and ¼ inch thick; be sure the longer edge is parallel to the edge of your work surface. Stir the roux a few times. Using a spatula or large spoon, spread about 4 tablespoons of the roux on the dough, leaving a ½-inch border around the edge. Sprinkle the salt over the roux. (It may seem like it's too much salt but it isn't.)

■ Starting from the longer edge of the rectangle, roll the dough into a cylinder, then seal the ends by pinching the edges together to create a seam. Cut the cylinder of dough into 8 equal segments.

■ Preheat the oven to 450 degrees F. Line a baking sheet with parchment paper. Set aside.

- Turn each segment of the dough so that the seam is on the bottom and the cut edge (where you see the coil of dough) is facing you. Roll out the dough into a rectangle about 5 inches long by 3½ inches wide and ¼ inch thick. Flip the rectangle so that the seam side is now facing up. Trifold the rectangle as if you were folding a letter. With the folded edge perpendicular to you, roll out the dough again into a rectangle about 5 inches long by 3½ inches wide. Repeat the trifold and set aside, with the flap facing down. Repeat with the remaining pieces of dough.

- Put the sesame seeds on a small plate. Brush a little water on the surface of each piece of dough. Dip the moistened sides into the sesame seeds. With the seed side up, roll each dough into a rectangle about 5 inches long by 3½ inches wide and ¼ inch thick. Place the bread on the prepared baking sheet. Repeat with the remaining dough. Bake for 15 minutes, then flip the breads and bake for 4 minutes more, or until the breads puff up and have a lightly browned color on the surface.

- Remove the breads from the oven and let them cool slightly before serving.

蛋 品

Eggs

Egg Bing with Onions and Bean Sprouts 227

Dad's Steamed Eggs with Tomatoes 228

Scrambled Eggs with Chinese Mustard Greens 231

Zucchini Egg Crepe 232

Wok-Fried Egg in Onion Oil 235

Home-Style Egg Foo Yung with Curry Gravy 236

Stir-Fried Eggs with Bean Thread Noodles and Wood Ear 238

Mu Shu Vegetables 239

If it weren't for my love of eggs, this book would've been naturally vegan. I didn't want to exclude egg dishes because a wok-fried egg with soy sauce is perfection, and I wanted to share a steamed-egg dish that my late father used to make when I was a little girl. These two dishes are so woven into my memories of a faraway time that it would feel like I was erasing those memories by not acknowledging them.

What I appreciate about eggs in general is their superpower to add just the right touch to any dish: a soft-cooked egg as a garnish for noodles, a fried egg on top of congee, egg blossoms to add heartiness and body to soup, scrambled to mix into a stir-fry or dumpling filling, an egg wash to seal spring rolls. Eggs have a way of taking care of you, especially in lean times.

I love the idea of having my own chickens for eggs, but I do not have enough patience to follow through. Instead, I buy eggs from my rancher friends, the Vojkovich family, who come to my nearby farmers' market every week. For nearly twenty years, we've bonded over their gorgeous eggs with orange yolks (and grass-fed meats). If I can't get to the farmers' market, I try to buy organic eggs from the grocery store. For such an elemental ingredient, I do what I can to get the best available.

In the pages that follow, I've reprised the wok-fried egg that I shared in my first book but with an onion-oil variation. I've also included a few other go-to egg preparations that I hope can inspire further explorations for incorporating eggs into your dishes. To kick off the chapter, you'll read about my father's steamed eggs with tomatoes. He would cook it occasionally back in the days after we'd just immigrated to the States. But after we got into the restaurant business, I don't ever remember him making this dish again. I don't know why. My only regret is that I never bothered to ask him the story behind his steamed eggs or the secrets to his recipe.

蛋餅＋綠豆芽及蔥花

Egg Bing with Onions and Bean Sprouts

MAKES 2 TO 4 SERVINGS

3 large eggs, beaten

¼ cup water

½ teaspoon kosher salt, divided

⅛ teaspoon white pepper powder

1 teaspoon vegetable oil

2 stalks green onions, cut into 2-inch segments

1 cup bean sprouts

Fried Shallots (page 132), for garnish (optional)

Chili sauce, for garnish (optional)

Chili Oil (page 207), for garnish (optional)

Suggested pairings: Mung Bean Congee (page 183) or Savory Soy Milk with Youtiao and Shao Bing (page 218)

In Mandarin, the term "bing" could describe any number of savory or sweet foods from cookies to flatbreads to omelets to filled meat pies. This egg *bing* is not quite a crepe or an omelet, but it resembles both. Instead of onions, you can use leeks or Chinese chives. (Fair warning: Chinese chives are extremely pungent and will overpower your refrigerator.) Serve any time of day as part of a meal.

■ In a medium bowl, combine the eggs with the water, ¼ teaspoon of the salt, and the white pepper powder. Stir and set aside.

■ In an 8-inch nonstick or cast-iron skillet, heat the vegetable oil over medium heat until the surface of the oil starts to shimmer. Add the onions, bean sprouts, and the remaining ¼ teaspoon salt, and stir to combine. Cook for about 30 seconds. Add the egg mixture, swirling the pan as needed to coat the vegetables. Reduce the heat to low. Let brown for about 1 minute. Using a flexible spatula, carefully slide the spatula around the edge of the eggs to loosen. Once the surface of the egg is barely set and no longer looks wet, carefully fold the *bing* in half, then transfer to a plate. Top with garnishes.

ALTERNATIVE: To make zucchini *bing*, add 1 cup grated zucchini instead of the bean sprouts.

Dad's Steamed Eggs

with Tomatoes

MAKES 4 SERVINGS

For the eggs:

3 large eggs, well beaten

1 cup water

For the sauce:

1 teaspoon vegetable oil

1 cup diced fresh tomatoes

1 stalk green onion, finely chopped

2 tablespoons soy sauce

¼ cup water

½ teaspoon sugar

¼ teaspoon sesame oil

⅛ teaspoon white pepper powder

Suggested pairings: Gai Lan with Oyster Mushrooms (page 148) and Taiwanese Cabbage with Garlic and Chili (page 142)

When we first came to the States, my father was studying for his graduate degree. He'd attend university courses during the day, then tag-team with my mother, who would go to work in the evenings. He'd study a bit and then have dinner ready by the time my mother could take her meal break. She'd jet home, the four of us would eat dinner, and then she'd jet back to work. I was about four years old at the time. There are two meals that I remember distinctly from that period: one was when my parents would splurge on snow crab, which at the time was a rare occasion, and the other was when my father would make steamed eggs. By the time I got into cookbook writing, my father had long passed and it was too late to ask him for his recipe. What follows is my interpretation from a memory.

■ To make the eggs, set up a steamer and bring the water to boil over high heat. Combine the eggs and 1 cup water in a heatproof bowl that fits in the steamer. When the steamer is ready, steam the eggs for 15 minutes.

■ To make the sauce, you can use a wok or a skillet. Heat the vegetable oil over medium-high heat for 10 to 15 seconds. Add the tomatoes and onion. Cook, stirring, for 1 to 2 minutes, or until the tomatoes have released some of their juice. Add the soy sauce, water, and sugar, and stir to combine. Let simmer for about 1 minute. Add the sesame oil and white pepper powder, then give it one last stir. Turn off the heat and cover with a lid to keep warm.

■ When the eggs are done steaming, carefully remove the dish and place on a trivet or a plate. Using a spoon, gently break the surface of the egg to create a few divots. Spoon the sauce over the eggs. Serve while steaming hot.

芥菜炒蛋

Scrambled Eggs
with Chinese Mustard Greens

MAKES 1 SERVING

1 teaspoon vegetable oil

¼ cup chopped Chinese mustard greens

1 stalk green onion, finely chopped

2 large eggs, beaten

¼ teaspoon kosher salt, divided

Scant ⅛ teaspoon white pepper powder, or to taste

Suggested pairing: Mung Bean Congee (page 183)

I don't usually make scrambled eggs. But there's something about the bitter greens and the white pepper powder that needs the straightforwardness of scrambled eggs. You can easily scale this up by adding extra greens and extra eggs. For a quick breakfast, I'll eat just the eggs. If I have a little more time, I'll eat the eggs with a bowl of plain congee.

▪ Heat a nonstick skillet over medium heat. Add the oil and heat until the surface starts to shimmer. Add the greens, onion, and ⅛ teaspoon of the salt, and stir to combine. Continue stirring for about 30 seconds. Add the eggs and swirl to coat. Reduce the heat to low. Season with the remaining salt and the white pepper powder. Gently scramble the eggs with a rubber spatula. Cook for 30 to 60 seconds, depending on your preferred doneness. Serve with toasted Shao Bing (page 222) or regular toast, and soy sauce with chili sauce, as desired.

SIMPLE CONGEE

Usually, if I have leftover rice, a simple congee or fried rice are ideal ways to use it up. To make a simple congee, combine 2 cups cooked rice with enough water to cover by ½ inch in a medium pot. Bring to a low boil over medium-high heat, then reduce the heat to low and simmer for 20 to 40 minutes, depending on how thick you prefer the rice.

節瓜攤餅

Zucchini Egg Crepe

MAKES 2 CREPES

1 cup grated zucchini

¾ teaspoon kosher salt, divided

1 tablespoon all-purpose flour

3 large eggs, beaten

¼ cup water

1 tablespoon vegetable oil

2 tablespoons fried shallots

Suggested pairing: Pickled Cucumber in Soy Sauce (page 244)

This won't make a dent in your zucchini harvest, but it's a simple way to showcase this prolific squash. My mother used to make these egg crepes as a snack for us that we could eat as we transitioned from shifts at our family restaurant. Or, she'd make them to serve with congee for breakfast. On their own, zucchini don't excite me. But in this preparation, the shredded zucchini take on a new dimension. I've taken the liberty of adding a sprinkle of fried shallots. Store-bought is totally fine, or you can make your own (page 232).

■   In a medium bowl, combine the grated zucchini with ½ teaspoon of the salt. Mix well and let sit for 5 to 10 minutes. Stir in the flour to coat. Add the eggs and water and mix well.

■   Heat a 9-inch nonstick or cast-iron skillet over medium-low heat for about 1 minute. Swirl in the oil and heat until the surface of the oil starts to shimmer. Add half of the egg-zucchini mixture and swirl the pan to coat the surface with the batter. Cook for about 1 minute. Using a flexible spatula, carefully slide it under the edge of the crepe, shimmying it around the pan to loosen. Once the surface of the batter is just set, remove the pan from the heat. Carefully slide the crepe out of the pan and onto a plate. Alternatively, you can fold the crepe in half before transferring to a plate. It's all right if the crepe breaks; it's not meant to be perfect. Repeat with the remaining batter and stack the finished crepe on top of the first.

■   To finish, sprinkle on the remaining ¼ teaspoon salt and the fried shallots before serving.

蔥油煎蛋

Wok-Fried Egg in Onion Oil

MAKES 1 SERVING

2 teaspoons vegetable oil

1 stalk green onion, cut into 2-inch segments

1 large egg

¼ to ½ teaspoon soy sauce, to taste

1 slice toast, for serving

If you have my first book, you know how much I love wok-fried egg. The crispy, bubbly edges plus the brininess of the soy sauce mixed with egg yolk are superb. Here, I wanted to add another layer of flavor by infusing the cooking oil with green onions. Toast or congee are perfect accompaniments.

▪ Preheat a wok over medium heat for about 30 seconds. Add the oil and heat for 5 seconds, or until it starts to shimmer. Add the onion and stir-fry for about 30 seconds. Turn off the heat and remove the onion, but leave the oil. If the onion isn't too charred, you can save it to serve with the egg. Otherwise, discard.

▪ Crack the egg into a small bowl, without breaking the yolk. Heat the wok over medium heat. Once the oil comes back to temperature—which shouldn't take long, since the wok should still be hot—carefully pour the egg into the oil. Let the bottom brown for 30 seconds, or until you see the edges of the egg white start to turn golden. Gently flip the egg. Cook until the egg yolk reaches the desired doneness, 30 to 60 seconds. Transfer to a plate and drizzle on the soy sauce. Serve with toast.

Home-Style Egg Foo Yung

with Curry Gravy

MAKES 2 OMELETS

For the gravy:

1½ tablespoons vegetable oil

1½ tablespoons all-purpose flour

1 teaspoon curry powder

1 cup water, plus 1 to 2 tablespoons more as needed

1 teaspoon black bean garlic sauce

1½ teaspoons soy sauce

For the omelets:

1½ cups bean sprouts, roughly chopped

2 stalks green onions, finely chopped

1 cup shredded Taiwanese cabbage or regular green cabbage

½ cup roughly chopped mushrooms, such as oyster, beech, or cremini

½ teaspoon kosher salt

⅛ teaspoon white pepper powder

4 large eggs, beaten

Vegetable oil, for frying

Finely chopped green onions, for garnish (optional)

Suggested pairing: Yu Choy with Fried Shallots (page 132)

Egg foo yung is basically a fluffy omelet with gravy. To get the eggs to puff up, they're gently deep fried in a giant wok. If you don't do much deep frying, this can be a barrier. So I offer two methods to make the omelet: shallow fry or deep fry. If you prefer a plain brown gravy, skip the curry powder.

■ To make the gravy, heat the oil in a small or medium pot over medium heat until the surface shimmers. Sprinkle the flour and curry powder in the oil, and stir with a whisk to combine. Add the 1 cup water, black bean garlic sauce, and soy sauce. Whisk to combine. Let the sauce come to a simmer, whisking occasionally to help it thicken. If it becomes too thick, you can add 1 to 2 tablespoons more water and whisk. The gravy should be thick but still pourable. Remove from heat and set aside, covered.

■ To make the omelets, in a large bowl, combine the bean sprouts, onions, cabbage, mushrooms, salt, and white pepper powder. Use tongs to combine. Add the eggs and mix again to incorporate. Set aside.

■ For the shallow-fry method: In a small skillet (about 8 inches), heat ½ cup vegetable oil over medium heat until the surface of the oil starts to shimmer. Scoop about 1 cup of the egg mixture and carefully pour into the center of the pan and spread it out like a pancake. Turn the heat to medium low. Fry for 1 to 2 minutes, or until lightly browned. Carefully flip the egg to cook the other side for another 1 to 2 minutes. Transfer to a platter and repeat with the remaining egg mixture. When you are cooking the last omelet, reheat the gravy over low heat, stirring as needed.

■ For the deep-fry method: Fill a large Dutch oven at least one-third full with vegetable oil and heat over medium heat to 325 degrees F. Line a platter with paper towels and set aside. Using a heatproof ladle, slowly tip a ladleful of egg mixture into the oil. Continue doing this with as many omelets as will comfortably float in the oil without crowding. Fry for 1 to 2 minutes, or until the bottom is golden. Flip the omelet to repeat on the other side. Transfer the browned omelets to drain on the platter. When you are cooking the last omelet, reheat the gravy over low heat, stirring as needed.

■ To serve, arrange the omelets on serving plates. Spoon the gravy over the eggs. Top with chopped green onions.

Stir-Fried Eggs

with Bean Thread Noodles and Wood Ear

MAKES 4 SERVINGS

3 teaspoons vegetable oil, divided

2 large eggs, beaten

1 stalk green onion, cut into 2-inch segments

½ cup bean sprouts

¼ cup wood ear mushrooms, soaked in warm water for 30 minutes and cut into ¼-inch-thick pieces

1 bundle bean thread noodles, soaked in warm water for 15 minutes and halved

¼ cup water

1 tablespoon soy sauce

½ teaspoon sesame oil

Steamed mu shu pancakes (optional; see Note)

Suggested pairing: Taiwanese Cabbage with Garlic and Chili (page 142)

Stir-frying bean thread noodles can be tricky because they stick so easily. You have to have enough oil to coat the surface of your wok and you also have to work fast. But it's so good and worth a few heightened seconds of cooking. While this recipe calls for mu shu pancakes as an accompaniment, you can also serve this dish with rice or eat it on its own as a noodle dish. It's up to you and what you're craving in the moment.

■ Preheat a wok over medium heat until wisps of smoke rise from the surface. Add 1 teaspoon of the vegetable oil and heat until it starts to shimmer. Add the eggs and scramble, cooking until the curd is just set, 1 to 2 minutes. Turn off the heat and transfer the eggs to a small dish and set aside. Wipe the wok clean.

■ Turn the heat to medium, and swirl in the remaining 2 teaspoons vegetable oil, making sure to coat the sides. Use a wok spatula to help spread the oil around as needed. Add the green onions, bean sprouts, and mushrooms, and stir-fry for about 30 seconds. Add the eggs, bean thread, water, and soy sauce. Stir-fry actively for 1 to 2 minutes to combine and to keep the noodles from sticking. If needed, reduce the heat to medium low. Once the noodles have softened and turn dark from the soy sauce, it's done. Turn off the heat. Add the sesame oil and give it one last stir. Serve with rice or with steamed mu shu pancakes.

NOTE: You can find store-bought mu shu pancakes in the freezer aisle of Asian markets. These are the same pancakes you use for Mu Shu Vegetables (page 239). They resemble flour tortillas but are thinner. Defrost the pancakes and steam them per the package instructions. The shortcut: Wrap 4 pancakes in a clean tea towel. Spritz some water on the towel to help create some steam and microwave for 30 seconds at a time until soft.

素木須

Mu Shu Vegetables

MAKES 4 SERVINGS

3 teaspoons vegetable oil, divided

2 large eggs, beaten

2 tablespoons water

1½ tablespoons sweet bean sauce

1 tablespoon hoisin sauce, plus more for serving

1 tablespoon soy sauce

8 store-bought mu shu pancakes, defrosted (see Note on page 238 for the microwave trick)

2 stalks green onions, cut into 2-inch segments

4 cups loosely packed, thinly sliced green cabbage

½ cup julienned carrots

1 cup bean sprouts

¼ teaspoon sesame oil

⅛ teaspoon white pepper powder

Suggested pairing: Ginger-Red Date Broth (page 110)

Even though we served mu shu (pork, chicken, shrimp, or vegetables) on the menu at our restaurant, it wasn't something we ate ourselves. I think it was mostly because it was an Americanized dish and my parents didn't have a connection to it in a way that would make them crave it. But it was a popular dish among our customers, and I'd sometimes look at the platters of mu shu heading out into the dining room with envy. Occasionally, my mother would make some on request. I loved the steaming-hot mu shu pancakes and filling and rolling them like burritos. Each bite was a happy moment.

■ Preheat a wok over medium heat until wisps of smoke rise from the surface. Add 1 teaspoon of the vegetable oil and heat until it starts to shimmer. Add the eggs and scramble them, cooking until the curd is just set, 1 to 2 minutes. Turn off the heat and transfer the eggs to a small dish and set aside. Wipe the wok clean.

■ In a small bowl, combine the water, sweet bean sauce, hoisin sauce, and soy sauce. Set aside.

■ Set up your steamer (see page 52) to steam the pancakes. Steam for 5 to 7 minutes, or until heated through and softened.

■ While the pancakes are steaming, heat the wok over high heat until wisps of smoke rise from the surface. Add the remaining 2 teaspoons vegetable oil and the green onions, and stir-fry for 10 to 15 seconds. Add the cabbage, carrots, bean sprouts, and eggs, and stir to combine. Add the sauce mixture and stir-fry for 1 to 2 minutes, or until the cabbage has softened. Add the sesame oil and white pepper powder, and toss again to combine. Turn off the heat and transfer to a serving dish. Serve with the pancakes on the side and hoisin sauce. Fill and roll like a burrito.

沙拉 ＋ 醬菜

Salads and Pickles

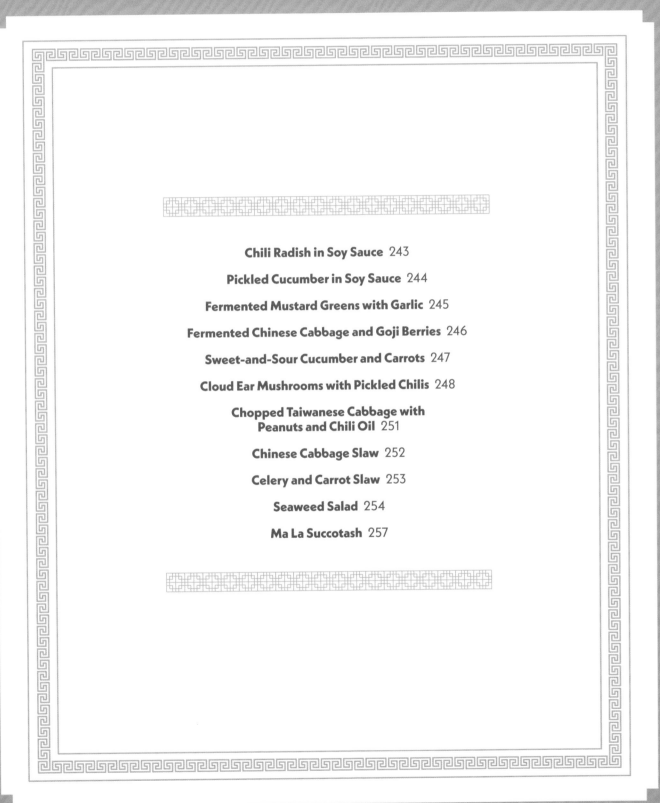

Chili Radish in Soy Sauce 243

Pickled Cucumber in Soy Sauce 244

Fermented Mustard Greens with Garlic 245

Fermented Chinese Cabbage and Goji Berries 246

Sweet-and-Sour Cucumber and Carrots 247

Cloud Ear Mushrooms with Pickled Chilis 248

**Chopped Taiwanese Cabbage with
Peanuts and Chili Oil** 251

Chinese Cabbage Slaw 252

Celery and Carrot Slaw 253

Seaweed Salad 254

Ma La Succotash 257

A recipe's marquee ingredient isn't always the one that steals the show. It could be a spice, a sauce, a condiment, or a pickle that ties a dish together or that balances the dish with a contrasting flavor. If you've ever explored the aisles of a Chinese market, the shelves upon shelves of pickled or fermented products are dizzying. Every trip to the market seems to reveal a new jar of pickled ingredients in unexpected combinations. I've started to notice the evolution of the offerings from the basics, such as cucumber or radish in soy sauce, to contemporary, Western-influenced intersections, such as the inclusion of truffles. Name a vegetable or fungus (or dried seafood) and it's likely represented on the shelf: bamboo shoots, wood ear, celtuce, cucumber, radish, cabbage, mustard greens, and so many types of chili.

These intensely flavored condiments pair perfectly with rice, congee, noodles, steamed buns, and so forth. They can be the amuse-bouche that gets the juices flowing and they can be the counterpoint in a stir-fry or soup. I have been known to eat pickles straight from the jar—sometimes sacrificing my stomach for the instant gratification. I'm not one to insist that you make all of your own pickles and ferments because that does take extra commitment. But I have a few straightforward recipes to get you started, if you so choose.

Unlike lettuce-based salads, these Chinese salads contain heartier ingredients that can handle some quality time with the dressings or marinades. The Seaweed Salad (page 254), if it's not devoured in the first sitting, will taste even better the next day. The Sweet-and-Sour Cucumber and Carrots (page 247) is something that a mom-and-pop Chinese restaurant might send out to all customers as a small gesture. It's not usually a high-value dish and yet it's surprisingly tasty.

Chili Radish in Soy Sauce

MAKES ABOUT 1 PINT

¾ to 1 pound daikon radish or Korean mu radish, peeled and cut into ¼-by-2-inch strips

½ cup water, plus more as needed

⅓ cup soy sauce

1 teaspoon chili bean sauce

2 teaspoons sesame oil

¼ teaspoon sugar

Suggested pairings: Mung Bean Congee (page 183), Savory Soy Milk (page 218), or Vegetable Noodle Soup (page 191)

When I was a girl, my favorite part of having congee was eating the Lan Chi brand preserved chili radish in soy sauce. I loved the briny, spicy, crunchy radish strips. Even though I had to drink a lot of water to tame the intensity, I couldn't stop eating them. At some point, my favorite Asian markets stopped carrying the product and I haven't found another brand that quite hits the same notes and takes me back to childhood. This version of chili radish in soy sauce is a quick pickle. You can eat the radish after a day, but it tastes better after a few days. The longer it's in the sauce, the more the flavor will permeate.

■ Place the daikon strips in a pint- or quart-size canning jar, depending on the amount of daikon you have. In a small bowl, combine the water, soy sauce, chili bean sauce, oil, and sugar. Pour over the daikon, making sure all the strips are submerged. Put the lid on and let marinate in the refrigerator for 1 to 2 days before eating. The daikon will keep for several months in the refrigerator as long as you use clean utensils to dish out the radish strips.

醬醃小黃瓜

Pickled Cucumber in Soy Sauce

MAKES 1 QUART

1½ cups water

½ cup soy sauce

4 tablespoons unseasoned rice vinegar

2 teaspoons sugar

1 teaspoon black bean garlic sauce

2 teaspoons sesame oil

1 teaspoon chili sauce (optional)

1 pound Persian or Japanese cucumber, cut into ½-inch-thick by 3-inch-long pieces

Suggested pairings: Mung Bean Congee (page 183) or Zucchini Egg Crepe (page 232)

Across Asian cultures, soy sauce pickles are common. Soy sauce itself is a fermented product, which adds great flavor to the vegetables. For this recipe, look for Persian cucumbers, which have a thin skin. The so-called "cocktail" cucumbers that you find in some stores also work well. If you can find Japanese cucumber, that would be great too.

■   In a medium pot, combine the water, soy sauce, vinegar, sugar, black bean garlic sauce, oil, and chili sauce. Bring to a boil, reduce the heat to medium low, add the cucumbers, and let simmer for 2 to 3 minutes. Turn off the heat. Using clean tongs, transfer the cucumbers into a sterilized 1-quart canning jar with a lid (it could be fresh out of the dishwasher). Using a ladle, add the liquid to the jar, making sure to submerge the cucumbers. Seal with the lid and set aside on the counter to cool to room temperature. Store in the refrigerator for 2 to 3 days before opening. The pickles should keep in the refrigerator for up to 2 months.

蒜香醃酸菜

Fermented Mustard Greens with Garlic

MAKES 1 PINT

1 cup room temperature water

1 tablespoon plus 1 teaspoon kosher salt

¾ pound Chinese mustard greens (*gai choy*), trimmed, cored, and sliced ¼ inch thick; reserve the core

2 cloves garlic, finely chopped

Suggested pairings: Flaky Ribbon Pancakes (page 89) or Mian Pian Soup (page 113)

Traditionally, the mustard greens are sun-dried and then fermented, which transforms the pungent vegetable into a tender pickle. Sun-drying is not so easy to do for many people. I live in Seattle, where it's nearly impossible to rely on consistent sun and warmth. The resulting greens in this method are nicely fermented, but they still have some crunch and don't look as shriveled. It's not better or worse, just differently tasty.

■ In a small bowl, combine the water and the 1 teaspoon salt. Stir to dissolve.

■ Put the sliced mustard greens in a medium bowl and add the 1 tablespoon salt. Using clean hands, work the salt in. Grab a handful of the greens at a time and give them a light squeeze. Repeat for 1 to 2 minutes until you have a pool of bright green juice in the bottom of the work bowl. Add the garlic and work it in.

■ Pack the greens as tightly as you can into a sterilized pint jar. Add the juices from the bowl. Using the reserved core, press the greens down to get rid of any air bubbles and to make sure the leaves are fully submerged in the liquid. Wedge the core in the top of the jar to help keep the greens submerged and, if needed, add some of the salt water to top it off. Leave about ¾-inch headspace at the neck of the jar. Seal with the lid so that it's firm but not so tight that the gases can't escape. Set the jar out of the direct sunlight in a spot in your kitchen where the temperature is steady. Let ferment for 7 to 10 days before eating. After opening, store the jar in the refrigerator.

Fermented Chinese Cabbage and Goji Berries

MAKES 1 PINT

1 cup room temperature water

1 tablespoon plus 1 teaspoon kosher salt

¾ pound Chinese cabbage, trimmed, cored, and sliced ¼ inch thick; reserve the core

2 teaspoons goji berries

Suggested pairings: Winter Melon with Smoked Salt (page 169) or Egg Bing with Onions and Bean Sprouts (page 227)

Chinese cabbage takes on a different character when fermented with the sweet-tart flavor of goji. The goji berries add a pop of color in the jar too. Serve this with rice or congee, or as a preamble to a meal. If you want to add a hint of spice, you can mix in ½ teaspoon red pepper flakes when you're packing the jar.

■ In a small bowl, combine the water and the 1 teaspoon salt. Stir to dissolve.

■ Put the sliced cabbage in a medium bowl and add the 1 tablespoon salt. Using clean hands, work the salt in. Grab a handful of the cabbage at a time and give it a firm squeeze. Repeat for 1 to 2 minutes until you have a pool of clear juice in the bottom of the work bowl. Add the goji berries and mix well.

■ Pack the cabbage as tightly as you can into a sterilized pint jar. Add the juices from the bowl. Using the reserved core, press the cabbage down to get rid of any air bubbles and to make sure the leaves are fully submerged in the liquid. Wedge the core in the top of the jar to help keep the leaves submerged and, if needed, add some of the salt water to top it off. Leave about ¾-inch headspace at the neck of the jar. Seal with the lid so that it's firm but not so tight that the gases can't escape. Set the jar out of the direct sunlight in a spot in your kitchen where the temperature is steady. Let ferment for 7 to 10 days before eating. After opening, store the jar in the refrigerator.

糖醋涼拌胡蘿蔔小黃瓜

Sweet-and-Sour Cucumber and Carrots

MAKES ABOUT 1 QUART

½ cup sugar

1 cup water

½ cup unseasoned rice vinegar

1 pound Persian or Japanese cucumber, sliced in half lengthwise and cut into ½-inch-thick slices

1 cup thinly sliced carrot coins

½ teaspoon kosher salt

Suggested pairings: Sweet Corn Soup (page 123) or Eggplant with Black Bean Garlic Sauce (page 170)

When my family first opened our Chinese restaurant, we included this quick pickle as an accompaniment to every lunch special. We had to make buckets of it. One of my jobs was to peel stripes on the outside of the cucumber and then scoop the seeds out of the middle. When sliced, the thick segments had a pretty effect from being partially peeled. Here, I've taken the liberty of using the tender Persian cucumber, which doesn't need to have the seeds removed.

▪ In a small pot, combine the sugar, water, and vinegar and bring to a boil over medium-high heat. Stir to dissolve the sugar. Once the mixture comes to a boil, reduce the heat to low and continue to simmer until the sugar has completely dissolved. This shouldn't take more than 2 to 3 minutes. Set aside and let cool to room temperature.

▪ In the meantime, combine the cucumber and carrots in a large bowl. Sprinkle on the salt and mix well to combine. Let sit while the dressing cools. Once cool, add the dressing to the vegetables. Stir well to combine. Cover the bowl and chill overnight, stirring once before going to bed. The next day, taste the cucumber. If needed, stir again and continue to marinate for a few more hours. Serve as an appetizer bite or as an accompaniment to a meal.

Cloud Ear Mushrooms

with Pickled Chilis

MAKES 4 TO 6 SERVINGS

6 cups water, for blanching

2 teaspoons kosher salt

¾ ounce cloud ear mushrooms (roughly ½ cup dried), soaked in warm water for 30 minutes

3 tablespoons soy sauce

2 teaspoons vinegar (see Note)

1 teaspoon (store-bought) pickled red chili pepper; alternatively, use fresh, sliced Thai bird chili

1 teaspoon Chili Oil (page 207)

1 teaspoon sesame oil

1 stalk green onion, finely chopped

2 heaping tablespoons chopped fresh cilantro

Suggested pairings: Simply Steamed Baby Bok Choy (page 160) and Simple Vegetable Fried Rice (page 193)

I prefer the smaller cloud ear fungus than wood ear for this dish so they don't have to be cut. It makes for a better mouthfeel and presentation. If you can't find cloud ear, then regular wood ear works fine. Just make sure to cut the larger pieces into roughly one-inch chunks and discard the white "stump" where the fungus is cut during harvest. When shopping for cloud ear, look for these characters on the packaging: 雲耳 (traditional Chinese) or 云耳 (simplified Chinese).

■ In a medium pot, bring the water and salt to a boil over high heat. Add the mushrooms, reduce the heat to medium low, and let simmer for 2 to 3 minutes. Drain the mushrooms in a colander and rinse with cold water until they are no longer hot to the touch. Let rest in the colander for a few minutes to drain any excess water.

■ In a small bowl, combine the soy sauce, vinegar, chili pepper, chili oil, and sesame oil. Transfer the mushrooms to a medium bowl. Add the sauce mixture and toss well to combine. If you have time, let the salad marinate in the sauce for 30 minutes and up to overnight. Top with the onion and cilantro.

NOTE: If you want a milder flavor, use unseasoned rice vinegar. For a stronger flavor, use Chinese black vinegar. For a hint of sweetness, use everyday balsamic vinegar.

Chopped Taiwanese Cabbage

with Peanuts and Chili Oil

MAKES ABOUT 2 SERVINGS

¾ pound Taiwanese cabbage, cut into 1-inch squares

½ teaspoon kosher salt

½ cup Huang Fei Hong Hot Chilli Pepper Peanuts (available in large Chinese markets) or roasted salted peanuts

2 tablespoons chili oil

Suggested pairings: Lucky 8 Stir-Fry (page 154) or Fried Brown Rice with Oyster Mushrooms and Greens (page 180)

The cabbage is salted, which helps to bring out the natural sweetness. The spicy peanuts make all the difference because they're seasoned with Sichuan peppercorns. So, if you can, look for the Huang Fei Hong peanuts. Chili oil can vary in spice level, so adjust the amount accordingly. If you can't get Taiwanese cabbage, you could substitute with regular green cabbage.

■ Put the cabbage into a large bowl. Sprinkle on the salt and rub it into the leaves of the cabbage, lightly squeezing fistfuls to bruise the leaves a bit. Continue to do this for about 1 minute. Add the peanuts and the chili oil. Using a spoon or tongs, thoroughly mix the ingredients together. Cover the bowl and let marinate for 1 to 2 hours, or until the cabbage has released some of its liquid and the flavors have come together. You can taste and give the mixture a toss a couple of times as it marinates. Serve right away or store in an airtight container in the refrigerator. This will keep in the refrigerator for several days.

涼拌大白菜絲

Chinese Cabbage Slaw

MAKES 4 TO 6 SERVINGS

2 cups thinly sliced Chinese cabbage, about ⅛ inch thick

½ cup shredded carrots

½ cup thinly sliced red, yellow, or orange bell pepper, about ⅛ inch thick

½ cup bean sprouts

1 teaspoon kosher salt

2 tablespoons soy sauce

1½ tablespoons unseasoned rice vinegar

1 teaspoon sesame oil

½ teaspoon sugar

½ cup roughly chopped fresh cilantro

Suggested pairings: Shen's Wok-Seared Broccoli with Jalapeños (page 152) or Sichuan Pepper Salt Fried Tofu (page 217)

I didn't grow up eating coleslaw and never acquired a taste for it. So, I didn't have positive associations with the term "slaw." But then I learned that slaw is a general term that could describe other types of slaw, including ones that use Chinese cabbage. I like the addition of carrots and sweet bell peppers for flavor and color. I don't like raw onions, but if you don't mind them, you can add about a stalk's worth of chopped green onions.

■ In a large bowl, combine the cabbage, carrots, bell pepper, and bean sprouts. Sprinkle with the salt and, using clean hands, work the salt into the vegetables by picking up handfuls and lightly squeezing. Do this repeatedly for 1 minute. Cover the bowl with plastic wrap and let rest on the counter for at least 10 minutes and up to an hour. Meanwhile, in a small bowl, combine the soy sauce, vinegar, oil, and sugar. Pour over the slaw and mix well. Add the cilantro, toss again, and serve.

中式芹菜涼拌胡蘿蔔絲

Celery and Carrot Slaw

MAKES ABOUT 2 CUPS

1 cup bias-cut celery slices, including the leaves, about ⅛ inch thick

1 cup julienned carrots

1½ tablespoons soy sauce

1 tablespoon unseasoned rice vinegar

1 teaspoon sesame oil

½ teaspoon chili oil (optional)

½ cup chopped fresh cilantro (optional)

Suggested pairings: Tofu Rolls (page 209) or Savory Mushrooms with Rice Powder (page 159)

Is it possible to be passive-aggressive when it comes to platters of carrots and celery sticks? I always have an urge to say that there are other ways to enjoy this classic pair. If you feel inclined, you can seek out Chinese celery, which is pungent and has long, skinny stalks. Be sure to rinse the Chinese celery thoroughly because a lot of dirt gets into the base of the stalks. If you want to add a hint of sweetness, use balsamic vinegar instead of the rice vinegar.

■ In a medium bowl, combine the celery and carrots and mix well. Add the soy sauce, vinegar, sesame oil, chili oil, and cilantro. Mix well. Let the mixture marinate for about 30 minutes before serving. This can hold in an airtight container in the refrigerator for several days.

Seaweed Salad

MAKES 4 TO 6 SERVINGS

About 2 cups sliced seaweed, soaked in warm water for 30 minutes to rehydrate

7 cups water, divided, for blanching

1 bundle bean thread noodles, soaked in warm water for 30 minutes to rehydrate

1 to 2 squares spiced tofu, cut into thin slivers (about 1 cup)

¼ cup soy sauce

1 teaspoon unseasoned rice vinegar

1 teaspoon sesame oil

Suggested pairings: Kung Pao Tofu Puffs (page 199) or Hot-and-Sour Soup with Dried Lily Flowers (page 114)

This recipe yields a generous amount of salad, but any leftovers can be saved for the next day. In fact, the longer it sits in the dressing, the more the flavors can come together. True story: I once made a batch and was letting it marinate on the counter. I returned later and found half of it gone because my mother and son had each snacked on some salad.

▪ Rinse the rehydrated seaweed in cool water to get rid of the natural slime that's on the surface of the seaweed. Let drain in a colander. Bring 4 cups of the water to a boil in a medium pot over high heat. Add the seaweed, reduce the heat to medium low, and let simmer for about 2 minutes. Remove from the heat and drain the seaweed in the colander. Rinse the seaweed in cold water until cool to the touch. Let sit in the colander to drain while you cook the noodles.

▪ Bring the remaining 3 cups water to a boil in the same pot over high heat. Reduce the heat to medium low, add the bean thread, and cook for 4 to 5 minutes, or until the noodles are translucent. Meanwhile, transfer the seaweed to a medium bowl so you can use the colander to drain the noodles. When the noodles are translucent, remove from the heat, drain, and rinse under cool running water to stop the cooking. Drain well.

▪ If the seaweed is in long strands, cut it to roughly 3-inch lengths. It won't be exact. Place in the bowl. Next, do the same with the noodles, cutting them into similar lengths. Place in the bowl with the seaweed. Add the tofu and toss to combine, making sure to break up the tangled pieces of seaweed and noodles. Then add the soy sauce, vinegar, and oil, and toss well to coat everything with the sauce. Serve right away or, better yet, let sit for at least 30 minutes to marinate.

麻辣彩豆

Ma La Succotash

MAKES ABOUT 2 CUPS

1 cup water

¾ cup frozen peas and carrots

½ cup frozen corn

½ cup frozen shelled edamame

¼ teaspoon kosher salt, plus more to taste

1 teaspoon soy sauce

¼ to ½ teaspoon ground toasted Sichuan peppercorns

½ teaspoon sesame oil

Suggested pairings: Braised Chinese Cabbage and Fried Shallots (page 111) or Crisp Vegetables with Lily Flowers (page 135)

If you need to practice your skills using chopsticks, this would be an ideal dish to test your ability. This is a good starter or side dish that blends the flavors of spring and summer with the hit of tingly Sichuan peppercorns. It's important that the peppercorns are fresh or you won't get the tingly effect. The colors pop and would brighten up the table, complementing any other dishes that have more earth tones in them.

■ Add the water to a medium pot and bring to a boil over medium-high heat. Reduce the heat to low. Add the peas and carrots, corn, edamame, and salt, and stir to combine. Cover with the lid and let steam for 3 to 5 minutes, stirring occasionally, or until the vegetables have cooked through. Strain the mixture and rinse with cool water to stop the cooking. Drain well and place the mixture in a medium bowl. Add the soy sauce, peppercorns, and oil. Stir well to combine. Taste and, if needed, adjust the seasoning by adding salt.

Acknowledgments

As I write this paragraph, it is the Saturday morning before my manuscript is due to my editor. The final few weeks before a book deadline are always intense, and I have engaged only as much as necessary with my family. My husband, Eric, is cleaning the kitchen after having made breakfast eggs on toast for me and is listening to David Sedaris's "MasterClass" on the kitchen sound system. I am wearing noise-canceling headphones (no music, just quiet), but I can hear him occasionally laughing at some turn of phrase that Sedaris is so adept at spinning. This domestic scene is the balance of our lives. I would rather have days filled with such mundane moments that are underpinned by an intimate knowing of one another and the safety to be who we are. Grand gestures can't compete. Thank you, Eric, for making it possible for me to strive the way I need to strive and building the home that anchors our family.

Thank you to Meilee and Shen for being yourselves. It's a pleasure to watch you evolve. I never know what nuggets of wisdom that I share actually resonate. Every time I start to worry, you will do or say something that demonstrates you heard me. I write to share my experience and teach people to cook. But, more importantly, I write so that you and your cousins know a piece of your history.

I am not literate in Chinese. Without my mother, Ellen, I would not have a lifeline to Chinese-only information that has been helpful in my research about ingredients and techniques. My mother has lived with us since 2005, and it has been our privilege to benefit from her life wisdom and a joy to watch her tend to her container garden. She has the magic touch to breathe life into languishing plants and even into the vegetable scraps that I have put in the compost bowl. More than once, she has taken a stem or trimming and produced a flourishing plant. It's the circle of life indeed. Thank you, Ma.

The year *Chinese Soul Food* was published was transformative. To have my first cookbook hit the shelves and be well received was the pinnacle. But 2018 also brought devastation to other parts of my professional life. It took more than a year to fully recover from a series of course-changing events. Kat Holmes saved me. She needed help with her own book launch and enlisted me to oversee this project. Through this work, I not only regained a sense of purpose, but I also got a coveted front-row seat to experience the knowledge and thinking about inclusive design for which Kat is an expert. Kat, you know how I feel. And, Don Holmes, thank you for supporting Kat's decision to work with me. Related, thank you to Aaron Woodman for your friendship during this particular time. In one of your *rare* moments of calm, you conveyed your belief in me with words I didn't know I needed to hear. Lunar New Year dinner for your crew and mine anytime! Good things beget good things, and the stabilizing effect of family relationships and friendships led me to a place where I could contemplate this new book and beyond.

Thank you to Susan Roxborough at Sasquatch Books for the easiest round of book proposal-to-contract I've experienced. Your trust in me and your compassion are meaningful. To the team at Sasquatch—Bridget Sweet, Tony Ong, and Diane Sinitsky—thank you for making me look good.

Clare Barboza: Of course you had to be my partner in this labor of love. Your willingness to push through weekend shoots and your attention to avoiding chopstick faux pas are so appreciated. The photos, oh, the photos. Heart emojis "to infinity and beyond." Dawn Smith: Our work was only partially represented in book one. Thank you for lending your expertise so that I could continue the story in book two. Special thanks to taste testers: Judy Simon, Angela Thyer, Sara Swett, Suji Park, Susan Denton, Kristin Agbalog, and Marc Erickson.

A POSTSCRIPT: Since I originally wrote the acknowledgments, the world came to a halt due to COVID-19. Social distancing, sheltering in place, and flattening the curve are all concepts we now know intimately. And then the police murdered George Floyd, which triggered massive, worldwide protests against police brutality and systemic racism. Despite the pandemic, people around the world have been marching, because Black Lives Matter. What lies ahead, I don't know. I want to mark this moment as a message to our future selves. Gratitude has carved new depths of meaning. Humanity has my faith. Thank you to all who share that faith.

Index

Note: Page numbers in *italic* refer to photographs.

A

Asian markets, shopping in, 15, 19
Asparagus Filling, Plant-Based "Beef" with, 77
Asparagus with Shiitake and Oyster
    Mushrooms, *162*, 163

B

Bamboo Shoots and Shiitake Mushrooms,
    Braised, *126*, 127
Baozi, Steamed Vegetable, *102*, 103–104
bean thread noodles
    Braised Chinese Cabbage and Fried
        Shallots, 111
    Seaweed Salad, 254, *255*
    Soup Dumplings, *94*, 95–96, *97*
    Spring Rolls, 92–93
    Steamed Vegetable Baozi, *102*, 103–104
    Stir-Fried Eggs with Bean Thread Noodles
        and Wood Ear, 238
    Taiwanese Cabbage and Tomato Soup with
        Bean Thread Noodles, 124, *125*
    Vegetarian Wonton Soup, 119–120, *121*
"Beef," Plant-Based, with Asparagus Filling, 77
"BLT" (Beech Mushrooms, Lettuce, and
    Tomato), 138, *139*
bok choy
    Seared Tofu with Baby Bok Choy, 214, *215*
    Simply Steamed Baby Bok Choy, 160, *161*
    trimming tips for baby bok choy, 160
Braised Tofu and Vegetables, 211
braises and soups, 106–127
broccoli, Chinese. *See gai lan*
Broccoli with Jalapeños, Shen's Wok-Seared,
    152
Broth, Ginger-Red Date, 110, *110*
Broth, Vegetable, 109
brussels sprouts, branches of, 145
Brussels Sprouts, Dry-Fried, 144, *145*

C

cabbage. *See* Chinese cabbage; Taiwanese
    cabbage
carrots
    Carrots and Celery with Spiced Tofu, 204,
        205
    Celery and Carrot Slaw, 253
    Hot-and-Sour Celery, Carrots, and Bean
        Sprouts, 150
    Ma La Succotash, *256*, 257
    Sweet-and-Sour Cucumber and Carrots,
        247
    Tofu, Peas, and Carrots, 212
cauliflower
    Cauliflower Rice with Eggplant and Gai
        Lan, 151
    Cauliflower with Edamame, Fried Onions,
        and Garlic, 166, *167*
    Savory Mushrooms with Rice Powder, 159
celery
    Carrots and Celery with Spiced Tofu, 204,
        205
    Celery and Carrot Slaw, 253
    Hot-and-Sour Celery, Carrots, and Bean
        Sprouts, 150
Chili Oil, 207
Chili Radish in Soy Sauce, 243
Chili Sauce, 120
Chilis with Cloud Ear Mushrooms, Pickled, 248,
    249
Chili-Shallot Jam, 174
Chinese broccoli. *See gai lan*
Chinese cabbage (napa cabbage)
    See also specific recipe
    Braised Chinese Cabbage and Fried
        Shallots, 111
    Chinese Cabbage Heart with Goji Berries,
        172, 173
    Chinese Cabbage Slaw, 252

Fermented Chinese Cabbage and Goji Berries, 246

Chinese cooking, vegetables in, 11–14

Chinese "Doughnuts" (Youtiao), 220, *221*

Chinese mustard greens (*gai choy*)

    Chinese Mustard Greens with Shishito Peppers, *146*, 147

    Fermented Mustard Greens with Garlic, 245

    Scrambled Eggs with Chinese Mustard Greens, *230*, *231*

Chinese Purple Seaweed and Tofu Soup, 116, *117*

chopsticks etiquette, 48

Cloud Ear Mushrooms with Pickled Chilis, 248, *249*

condiments. *See* sauces and flavorings

Congee, Mung Bean, *182*, 183

Congee, Simple, 231

cooking equipment, 47–55, *50–51*, *53*

cooking ingredients. *See* ingredients

cooking techniques. *See* techniques

cooking temperature and timing, 62–63

Corn and Edamame, Wok-Seared, *140*, 141

Corn Soup, Sweet, *122*, 123

Crispy Noodles, Hong Kong–Style, 194, *195*

cucumbers

    Cucumber and Wood Ear Mushrooms, 165

    Pickled Cucumber in Soy Sauce, 244

    Sweet-and-Sour Cucumber and Carrots, 247

    Vegetable Noodle Soup, *190*, 191

cutting techniques, 58–60, *59*

D

Da Lu Noodles, 192

Daikon, Braised, 115

Daikon Radish in Soy Sauce, Chili, 243

desserts, Chinese, 13

dim sum and small bites, 80–105

dipping sauces. *See* sauces and flavorings

Dough, Classic Dumpling, 72–73

Dough, Gluten-Free Dumpling, 74–75

"Doughnuts," Chinese (Youtiao), 220, *221*

dried ingredients, preparing, 56, 58

dumplings, 64–79

    Classic Dumpling Dough, 72–73

    cooking methods, 69–70

    Crystal Dumplings with Squash and Peas, *84*, 85–86, *87*

    Dumpling Code, 66–67

    Dumpling Dipping Sauce, 78, *79*

    Gluten-Free Dumpling Dough, 74–75

    making and storing, 68

    Plant-Based "Beef" with Asparagus Filling, 77

    pleating, *97*

    Soup Dumplings, *94*, 95–96, *97*

    store-bought wrappers, 73

    Tofu and Spinach Filling, 76

E

edamame

    Cauliflower with Edamame, Fried Onions, and Garlic, 166, *167*

    Ma La Succotash, *256*, 257

    Wok-Seared Edamame and Corn, *140*, 141

Egg Bing with Onions and Bean Sprouts, 227

Egg Foo Young, Home-Style, 236, *237*

Eggplant and Gai Lan, Cauliflower Rice with, 151

Eggplant with Black Bean Garlic Sauce, 170, *171*

eggs, 224–239

equipment, 47–55, *50–51*, *53*

F

Fermented Chinese Cabbage and Goji Berries, 246

Fermented Mustard Greens with Garlic, 245

Flatbread, Sesame (Shao Bing), 222–223

Fried Brown Rice with Oyster Mushrooms and Greens, 180, *181*

Fried Rice, Simple Vegetable, 193

G

gai choy. See Chinese mustard greens
gai lan (Chinese broccoli)
    Cauliflower Rice with Eggplant and Gai Lan, 151
    Gai Lan with Oyster Mushrooms, 148, *149*
    Gai Lan with Sesame Sauce, 164
garlic/ginger, in jars/tubes, 36
Ginger-Red Date Broth, 110, *110*
Ginger-Scallion Oil, 160
Gluten-Free Dumpling Dough, 74–75
Goji Berries, Chinese Cabbage Heart with, *172*, 173
Goji Berries, Fermented Chinese Cabbage and, 246

H

Hong Kong–Style Crispy Noodles, 194, *195*
Hot-and-Sour Celery, Carrots, and Bean Sprouts, 150
Hot-and-Sour Soup with Dried Lily Flowers, 114

I

ingredients
    combining, 60–61
    Core Pantry, 16–28, *17–18*, *22*, *25–26*
    fresh vegetables and other perishables, 28–41, *29–30*, *34*, *38–39*
    meat or seafood, adding, 134
    preparing dried ingredients, 56, 58
    preparing produce, 58–60, *59*
    shopping for, 15, 19
    size variability, 21
    soy sauce, *42*, 43–46

K

Kung Pao Tofu Puffs, 199–200, *201*

L

Leeks and Cabbage, Spiced Tofu with, *202*, 203
lily flowers, dried
    Crisp Vegetables with Lily Flowers, 135
    Da Lu Noodles, 192
    Hot-and-Sour Soup with Dried Lily Flowers, 114
    Lucky 8 Stir-Fry, 154, *155*
Lotus Leaf, Sticky Rice in, *98*, 99–100, *101*
Lucky 8 Stir-Fry, 154, *155*
Lunar New Year, 153

M

Ma La Succotash, *256*, 257
Ma Po Tofu, Meatless, 206–207
meat or seafood, adding, 134
Mian Pian Soup, *112*, 113
mu shu pancakes, store-bought, 238
Mu Shu Vegetables, 239
Mung Bean Congee, *182*, 183
mushrooms
    Asparagus with Shiitake and Oyster Mushrooms, *162*, 163
    "BLT" (Beech Mushrooms, Lettuce, and Tomato), 138, *139*
    Braised Bamboo Shoots and Shiitake Mushrooms, *126*, 127
    Cloud Ear Mushrooms with Pickled Chilis, *248*, 249
    Cucumber and Wood Ear Mushrooms, 165
    Fried Brown Rice with Oyster Mushrooms and Greens, 180, *181*
    Gai Lan with Oyster Mushrooms, 148, *149*
    Savory Mushrooms with Rice Powder, 159
    Stir-Fried Eggs with Bean Thread Noodles and Wood Ear, 238

N

napa cabbage. *See* Chinese cabbage
noodles and rice, 176–195
    See also bean thread noodles

Mian Pian Soup, *112*, 113

O

Oil, Chili, 207
Oil, Ginger-Scallion, 160
Onion Oil, Wok-Fried Egg in, *234*, 235
Onions and Bean Sprouts, Egg Bing with, 227
oyster mushrooms
    Asparagus with Shiitake and Oyster
        Mushrooms, *162*, 163
    Fried Brown Rice with Oyster Mushrooms
        and Greens, 180, *181*
    Gai Lan with Oyster Mushrooms, 148, *149*

P

Pancakes, Flaky Ribbon, *88*, 89–90, *91*
pantry ingredients, 16–28, *17–18*, *22*, *25–26*
Pea Shoots, Ginger-Scallion, *136*, 137
peas
    Crystal Dumplings with Squash and Peas,
        84, 85–86, *87*
    Ma La Succotash, *256*, 257
    Tofu, Peas, and Carrots, 212
pickles and salads, 240–257
portion sizes, 11
pot sticker lace, 70, *71*
pot stickers, 70

R

Radish in Soy Sauce, Chili, 243
Red Bean Soup, 105
Red Date-Ginger Broth, 110, *110*
Rice, Cauliflower, with Eggplant and Gai Lan,
    151
rice and noodles, 176–195
    See also congee
Rice Cake Soup with Vegetables, 118
Rice Cake with Mixed Vegetables, 184, *185*
rice cookers, fancy, 179
Rice in Lotus Leaf, Sticky, *98*, 99–100, *101*
Rice Powder, Savory Mushrooms with, 159

Rice Vermicelli with Vegetables, *186*, 187
Rolls, Spring, 92–93
Rolls, Tofu, *208*, 209–210

S

salads and pickles, 240–257
sauces and flavorings
    Chili Oil, 207
    Chili Sauce, 120
    Chili-Shallot Jam, 174
    Dumpling Dipping Sauce, 78, *79*
    Ginger-Scallion Oil, 160
    Sichuan Pepper Salt, 217
    Sweet-and-Sour Sauce, 93
seafood or meat, adding, 134
seaweed
    Chinese Purple Seaweed and Tofu Soup,
        116, *117*
    Seaweed Salad, 254, *255*
    Vegetable Broth, 109
Shallot-Chili Jam, 174
Shao Bing (Sesame Flatbread), 222–223
shiitake mushrooms
    Asparagus with Shiitake and Oyster
        Mushrooms, *162*, 163
    Braised Bamboo Shoots and Shiitake
        Mushrooms, *126*, 127
Shishito Peppers, Chinese Mustard Greens
    with, *146*, 147
Sichuan Pepper Salt Fried Tofu, *216*, 217
Slaw, Chinese Cabbage, 252
Slaw, Tofu Ribbon, 213
Soup, Red Bean, 105
Soup, Vegetable Noodle, *190*, 191
Soup Dumplings, *94*, 95–96, *97*
soups and braises, 106–127
Soy Milk with Youtiao and Shao Bing, Savory,
    218–223, *219*, *221*
soy sauce, about, *42*, 43–46
Soy Sauce, Chili Radish in, 243
Soy Sauce, Pickled Cucumber in, 244
Spring Festival. *See* Lunar New Year
Spring Rolls, 92–93

Spring Rolls, Tofu, *208*, 209–210

Squash and Peas, Crystal Dumplings with, *84*, 85–86, *87*

steamed dishes, 156–175

Steamed Eggs with Tomatoes, Dad's, 228, *229*

Steamed Rice, 179

Steamed Vegetable Baozi, *102*, 103–104

steaming dumplings, tips for, 70

Sticky Rice in Lotus Leaf, *98*, 99–100, *101*

Stir-Fried Eggs with Bean Thread Noodles and Wood Ear, 238

Stir-Fried Noodles, Simple, 188, *189*

stir-fries, 128–155

Succotash, Ma La, *256*, 257

Sweet Potatoes with Chili-Shallot Jam, 174, *175*

Sweet-and-Sour Cucumber and Carrots, 247

Sweet-and-Sour Sauce, 93

T

Taiwanese cabbage
    Chopped Taiwanese Cabbage with Peanuts and Chili Oil, *250*, 251
    Home-Style Egg Foo Young, 236, *237*
    Spiced Tofu with Leeks and Cabbage, *202*, 203
    Taiwanese Cabbage and Tomato Soup with Bean Thread Noodles, 124, *125*
    Taiwanese Cabbage with Garlic and Chili, 142, *143*

techniques, 56–63
    combining ingredients, 60–61
    good habits, 57
    mastering heat, 62–63
    meat or seafood, adding, 134
    preparing ingredients, 56, 58–60, *59*

tofu, 196–223

Tofu and Chinese Purple Seaweed Soup, 116, *117*

Tofu and Spinach Filling, 76

tomatoes
    "BLT" (Beech Mushrooms, Lettuce, and Tomato), 138, *139*
    Dad's Steamed Eggs with Tomatoes, 228, *229*
    Taiwanese Cabbage and Tomato Soup with Bean Thread Noodles, 124, *125*

tools, 47–55, *50–51*, *53*

V

Vegetable Broth, 109

Vegetable Fried Rice, Simple, 193

Vegetable Noodle Soup, *190*, 191

W

wine, and Chinese food, 13

Winter Melon with Smoked Salt, *168*, 169

Wok-Fried Egg in Onion Oil, *234*, 235

woks, seasoning and maintaining, 55, *55*

Wonton Soup, Vegetarian, 119–120, *121*

wood ear mushrooms
    Crisp Vegetables with Lily Flowers, 135
    Cucumber and Wood Ear Mushrooms, 165
    Stir-Fried Eggs with Bean Thread Noodles and Wood Ear, 238

Y

Yam Leaf, Garlic, 131

Youtiao (Chinese "Doughnuts"), 220, *221*

Yu Choy with Fried Shallots, 132, *133*

Z

Zucchini Bing, 227

Zucchini Egg Crepe, 232, *233*

Conversions

VOLUME

UNITED STATES	METRIC	IMPERIAL
¼ tsp.	1.25 ml	
½ tsp.	2.5 ml	
1 tsp.	5 ml	
½ Tbsp.	7.5 ml	
1 Tbsp.	15 ml	
⅛ c.	30 ml	1 fl. oz.
¼ c.	60 ml	2 fl. oz.
⅓ c.	80 ml	2.5 fl. oz.
½ c.	125 ml	4 fl. oz.
1 c.	250 ml	8 fl. oz.
2 c. (1 pt.)	500 ml	16 fl. oz.
1 qt.	1 l	32 fl. oz.

LENGTH

UNITED STATES	METRIC
⅛ in.	3 mm
¼ in.	6 mm
½ in.	1.25 cm
1 in.	2.5 cm
1 ft.	30 cm

WEIGHT

AVOIRDUPOIS	METRIC
¼ oz.	7 g
½ oz.	15 g
1 oz.	30 g
2 oz.	60 g
3 oz.	90 g
4 oz.	115 g
5 oz.	150 g
6 oz.	175 g
7 oz.	200 g
8 oz. (½ lb.)	225 g
9 oz.	250 g
10 oz.	300 g
11 oz.	325 g
12 oz.	350 g
13 oz.	375 g
14 oz.	400 g
15 oz.	425 g
16 oz. (1 lb.)	450 g
1½ lb.	750 g
2 lb.	900 g
2¼ lb.	1 kg
3 lb.	1.4 kg
4 lb.	1.8 kg

TEMPERATURE

OVEN MARK	FAHRENHEIT	CELSIUS	GAS
Very cool	250–275	130–140	½–1
Cool	300	150	2
Warm	325	165	3
Moderate	350	175	4
Moderately hot	375	190	5
	400	200	6
Hot	425	220	7
	450	230	8
Very Hot	475	245	9

About the Author

Hsiao-Ching Chou is the author of this book's predecessor, *Chinese Soul Food*. She teaches everyday Chinese home cooking at schools in the Seattle area and on YouTube, and she is known for her always-sold-out pot sticker classes. Currently she serves as the chair of the James Beard Foundation's Book Awards Committee and volunteers as a member of the board of directors for the Ballard Food Bank. When she's not wearing her culinary hat, she makes her living  as a communications and marketing manager in the biomedical research industry. Chou lives in Seattle with her husband, two children, and her mother. Learn more at MyChineseSoulFood.com.

Printed in the United States of America

SASQUATCH BOOKS with colophon is a registered trademark of Penguin Random House LLC

25 24 23 22 21   9 8 7 6 5 4 3 2 1

Editor: Susan Roxborough
Production editor: Bridget Sweet
Designer: Tony Ong
Photographs and prop styling: Clare Barboza
Food styling: Hsiao-Ching Chou

Library of Congress Cataloging-in-Publication Data
Names: Chou, Hsiao-Ching, 1972- author.
Title: Vegetarian Chinese soul food : deliciously doable ways to cook greens, tofu, and other plant-based ingredients / Hsiao-Ching Chou ; photography by Clare Barboza.
Description: Seattle : Sasquatch Books, 2021. | Includes index.
Identifiers: LCCN 2020023121 (print) | LCCN 2020023122 (ebook) | ISBN 9781632173331 (hardcover) | ISBN 9781632173348 (ebook)
Subjects: LCSH: Cooking, Chinese. | Vegetarian cooking. | LCGFT: Cookbooks.
Classification: LCC TX724.5.C5 C57194 2021 (print) | LCC TX724.5.C5 (ebook) | DDC 641.5/636--dc23
LC record available at https://lccn.loc.gov/2020023121
LC ebook record available at https://lccn.loc.gov/2020023122

ISBN: 978-1-63217-333-1

Sasquatch Books
1904 Third Avenue, Suite 710
Seattle, WA 98101
SasquatchBooks.com